Snow Falling On Cedars

Jorge Consuegra

EXT. THE SUSAN MARIE, SHIP CHANNEL BANK - NIGHT
Fog. Penetrated only by sound. The LAPPING of sea at a drifting hull. Tendrils of mist part, revealing...
...a face. Strong and blond and handsome.

SUPERIMPOSE: SEPTEMBER 15, 1954
LONG ANGLE...from below, we watch CARL HEINE, high on the cross spar of his mast. He has pulled a SHUTTLE of TWINE from his rubber overalls, and is LASHING a LANTERN in the cloud of mist, as MAIN

TITLES BEGIN...
ANGLE...the tiny, meticulously neat cabin. Empty, silent. A tin
COFFEE CUP on the counter's edge. The battery well open, revealing two large BATTERIES in place. PAN to...
...the deck of this sturdy stern-picker. The fishing net stretched from the huge DRUM into the sea. Keep PANNING to the bow, where...
...Carl stands with his kerosene lantern and his air horn, watching as another BOAT comes slowly out of the mist. The silhouette of a
FISHERMAN, holding a long fishing GAFF. As fragments of fog part, we CLOSE on the figure's face, to see...
...his eyes. They are Asian. SMASH CUT to...

EXT. THE SUSAN MARIE, SHIP CHANNEL BANK - MORNING
Blinding sun. Our boat bobs lifeless on placid water. As CREDITS
CONTINUE, two figures slowly reel in the massive net. SHERIFF ART
MORAN is painfully thin, unimposing, methodical. Only the eyes reflect his disquiet. His young deputy, ABEL MARTINSON, cuts anxious looks between his mentor and the sea. As the net brings silvered salmon across the gunnel, CUT to...
...the cabin. Tidy as before. Only two things have changed.
CLOSE on the tin coffee cup, which now lies OVERTURNED on the floor. PAN above the open battery well, where a third MARINE
BATTERY now stands next to the wheel. CUT to...
...the stern, as the raveling net LIFTS from the water's surface...
...the face of Carl Heine. Turned to the sun. SMASH CUT to...

INT. CORONER'S LAB - DAY
WHITE fills the frame. A hand PULLS back the blanket-shroud revealing Carl's face. As CREDITS CONTINUE, tilt up to the coroner, HORACE WHALEY, gazing down. A shading of regret behind the professional mask. A series of QUICK CUTS...
...Whaley's hand pulls the SHUTTLE of TWINE from Carl's pocket...
...examines the open, empty KNIFE SHEATH at Carl's belt...
...Carl's wrist, its WATCH stopped at 1:47...
Whaley bends over Carl's body, presses on his solar plexus, watching pink FOAM rise from Carl's mouth and nose. And then.
He sees something more. His fingers gently pull back the hair from above Carl's left ear, to reveal...

...a skull wound. The bone caved in. Four inches across.

EXT. SAN PIEDRO ISLAND - DAY
Snow falling on cedars.

SUPERIMPOSE: DECEMBER 6.
The heavens descend softly onto our island. Exquisite, silent, hypnotic. An epic snowfall inspiring awe at our frailness against the limitless scope of nature. As CREDITS CONCLUDE, a series of

QUICK ANGLES...
...cars pirouetting, skating on their tires, past an abandoned school bus, where kids throw snowballs at is windows...
...Fisk's Hardware Center, its endless queue of orderly citizens waiting stoically for their snow shovels and kerosene...
...the harbor, with its moored fleet of tiny fishing vessels blanketed as if by volcanic ash, a pair of teenage lovers building a snowman at the edge of a dock, she pushes the boy into the water, and he rises laughing, steam rising from his clothes...
...undulating strawberry fields of pure white, untouched and flawless as the Sahara...
Finally, to a public building, cars gathering as best they can, people streaming up snow-laden steps to the entrance, and as we
FOLLOW them, SMASH CUT to...

INT. COURTROOM - DAY
CLOSE on impassive EYES. They are Asian. We have seen them before. PULL BACK to see...
KABUO MIYAMOTO. Early 30's, dark blue suit, clean shirt. He sits ramrod straight, utterly motionless, expressionless, the eye of a storm of movement in...
...the assembling COURTROOM. A packed gallery of buzzing locals, the scent of anticipation. A bank of REPORTERS and PHOTOGRAPHERS, cosmopolitan in attire, bearing themselves as jaded dignitaries from the civilized world. As we PAN their ranks...

ISHMAEL (V.O.)
It was the first murder trial on the island in thirty-one years.
...we look over the right shoulder of ISHMAEL CHAMBERS, early 30's, dark, a rugged, somber man jotting notes on a pad which rests on his right leg.

ISHMAEL (V.O.)
Our only newspaper was the San
Piedro Review, a four-page weekly that I operated alone.
He glances blandly at his nonchalant colleagues.

ISHMAEL (V.O.)
What, I wondered, could the Seattle boys know of the hearts of these people...

To the JURY BOX. Truck farmers, grocers, fishermen, in sober neckties. A waitress, a secretary, fisher wives in Sunday dresses.

ISHMAEL (V.O.)
Neighbors, sitting in judgement.
On their neighbor.
To the neighbor. The ramrod-still defendant.

ISHMAEL (V.O.)
Kabuo Miaymoto sat with the rigid grace of a Samurai warrior. As if detached from his own trial.
Ishmael writing on the pad balanced precariously on his knee, until...

ISHMAEL (V.O.)
Did he know how dangerous his demeanor could be? With this jury.
...it falls with a CLATTER of pages. He reaches with his right hand, replaces the pad on his thigh. Around him, CAMERAS are being swung to the ready. Ishmael looks to see...
...a slender WOMAN of refined beauty, entering the courtroom.
A few flashes POP, and Ishmael's right hand retrieves a venerable box camera from beneath his seat, as his notepad falls once more, unheeded.

ISHMAEL (V.O.)
Hatsue Miyamoto had been without her husband for 77 days.
Ishmael pivots, and we understand his struggle with the notepad.
For he is forced to rest his camera on the stump of his amputated left arm, its empty sleeve pinned at the elbow.

ISHMAEL (V.O.)
He was in jail. When his baby son learned to walk.
Through his VIEWFINDER, we see HATSUE take her place in the first row. And sensing her presence, her husband turns. Their eyes meet. A string of FLASHES...
But none from Ishmael. He hesitates. As if considering whether he will violate this woman's privacy. The camera lowers. HOLD on his face...

INT. COURTHOUSE CORRIDOR - DAY
MATCH CUT to Hatsue's face. Staring, impassive, empty. PULL BACK to see that she sits alone on a wooden bench by the courtroom door.
Her hands rest delicately on the purse in her lap. Her demeanor as removed from this place as is her husband's.

ISHMAEL (V.O.)
Earlier, I noticed her in the corridor.
PULL BACK to see him alone, in shadow. It is more than a notice.
Ishmael stares with fixed intensity at the motionless woman, as she gathers her thoughts.
A moment of decision. He approaches.

Stops, respectfully, at a distance which will not invade her personal space. And softer than we might have imagined...

ISHMAEL
Are you all right?
She turns her head only slightly. It is enough. Her voice quiet and firm at once...

HATSUE
Go away, Ishmael.
There is no anger. Only directness and resolve.

ISHMAEL
Please don't be like th...
HATSUE (softer)
Go away.

INT. COURTROOM - DAY
PAN the back of the courtroom. Twenty-four citizens of Japanese ancestry fill the last row, dressed in their most formal clothes.
Shades of Atticus Finch. As one, the Japanese-Americans watch...
...the prosecutor, ALVIN HOOKS, a crisp, even dapper man. There is a quickness about the eyes, a tendency to sharpness of manner, that he works carefully against...

HOOKS
...four inch gash, skull crushed, and your thought was, what...?
JUDGE FIELDING, tall and gray and rawboned, leans on his elbows, his eyelids droop slightly, a deceptive masking of keen attention.

HOOKS (O.S.)
That he...fell? Hit his head on the gunnel going over?
The witness is Sheriff Moran. He answers as if this were a sincere question. As if he had never heard it before.

MORAN
Well, Carl was six-four, went 235.
He was a grizzly bear and an able seaman...
Ishmael watching. Thinking on that.

MORAN (O.S.)
For him to just...go over. Crush his skull like that on the way in...
HOLD on Ishmael.

INT. TEAM BUS - DAY
Teenage BOYS in football uniforms. They ride with their helmets in their laps.

ISHMAEL (V.O.)

He was a mountain, all right.
Anchored the line for us little fellers.
CLOSE on Carl and Ishmael at 18, riding together. Ishmael, dark and rugged even then, is scarcely little. But dwarfed by the blond giant at his side, who glares out the window, at...

CARL
Chambers. Y'see the geese?
...snow geese landing in low flooded wheat. The grace of it holds both boys.

CARL
Picture'd be nice. In your pa's paper.
Ishmael nods absently. They stare, side-by-side.

ISHMAEL
Lucky I got the camera in my helmet.
They never look at each other. They never smile. But you can almost hear one in...

CARL
Careful, Chambers. That was almost a joke.

INT. COURTROOM - DAY
Hooks now stands with his polished shoe up on the witness podium.
Like chatting with the Sheriff across the back fence...

HOOKS
And you weren't there, when the coroner examined the wound.

MORAN
Nossir. I'd gone to tell the wid... to tell Mrs. Heine.
And his glance inevitably goes to the first row behind the prosecutor's table. Taking the glances of the jury with it.
SUSAN MARIE HEINE is pretty and blonde and full-bodied in her modest black dress. Composure and dignity. Against her grief.

EXT. HEINE HOME - DAY
Moran climbs from his vehicle, as Carl's young SONS dash around the corner of the house. Seeing the Sheriff, they stop cold. Silent, shirtless, barefoot.

MORAN
Hey there, men. Is your mother home a-tall?
He spits his Juicy Fruit into a wrapper. And as the younger boy nods across the distance...

SUSAN MARIE (O.S.)
Sheriff Moran, hullo.

She has appeared in the doorway, smiling, spittle-marked baby's diaper across her shoulder. And he smiles back. Tells the boys...

MORAN
You go on and play, now.
But they don't. So he follows into her entryway, closing the door behind him. And at the foot of her curving staircase...

SUSAN MARIE
What can I do for you, Sheriff,
Carl's not home y...

MORAN
That's...
Too quick. He stops himself. And she sees that.

MORAN

It's why I'm here. I'm afraid I have some...very bad news to tell you, the...worst...kind of news.
She looks at him, uncomprehending, the smile only beginning to fade, before...

MORAN

Carl died last night. In a fishing accident. In White Sand Bay.
She only blinks. As if translating the words from a foreign language.

SUSAN MARIE
No, Carl's fine, h...

MORAN

We found him, Mrs. Heine. Tangled in his net.
And with these words, a slack, blank look crosses her face, and she stumbles back one step, sitting down HARD on the bottom stair of her curved staircase.
He doesn't know what to do. She digs her elbows into her lap, and begins to rock, very slowly, wringing the diaper in her hands. Her face is more terrible than tears. It is frightened. She murmurs to herself, so that we can barely hear...

SUSAN MARIE
I told him this could happen.

INT. COURTROOM - DAY
CLOSE on Hooks, nodding. As if, slowly, digesting something in his mind.

HOOKS
So, no...immediate suspicion, no...general talk of enmity between the two.

MORAN

These are fishermen, Alvin. They don't talk at all to each other and less to me. Specially gossip.

EXT. DOCKS - DAY
Ishmael walking down the sunlit wharf. Purpose in his stride...

ISHMAEL (V.O.)
A gill-netter works through black nights with only himself to talk to. And learns to be silent.
They were lonely men and products of geography.
Up ahead, the Susan Marie has been brought to dock. Moran stands chatting with a knot of six or seven FISHERMEN.

ISHMAEL (V.O.)
...men who, on occasion, realized that they wished to speak, but couldn't.
As he arrives, Moran smiles a thin greeting. Not happy to see him.
Of course, neither is anyone else.

MORAN
Figure you'da heard by now.
Ishmael shakes his head in silent helplessness. WILLIAM GJOVAAG, a sunburned, big-bellied, tattooed gill-netter, clamps on his damp cigar butt.

GJOVAAG
You go fishing, it happens.
ISHMAEL (to Moran)
You see Susan Marie?

MORAN
I did. Boy.

ISHMAEL
Three kids. What's she going to do?
GJOVAAG (disgusted)
Well, what can she do? Jesus Christ.

ISHMAEL
Excuse me, Gjovaag.

GJOVAAG
I don't need to excuse nothin'.
Fuck you anyhow, Chambers.
Everybody laughs. It is all good-natured, sort of.

ISHMAEL (V.O.)
Like the Sheriff, I did not work the sea, and could never merit trust.

Or respect.

MARTY JOHANSSON
Sheriff's been askin' which boats followed Carl out last night...
MORAN (quickly)
Only to see if somebody talked to him out th...

ISHMAEL
So who talked to him? Out there.
Staring. At each other. Eye contact holds during...
JAN SORENSEN (heavy Danish)
So far, we figured the guys who went to Ship Channel Bank, was Jim Ferry,
Hardwell, Moulton, Miyamoto...
GJOVAAG (spits)
Japs.

MORAN
All right, look, if you see these boys...

GJOVAAG
Never saw you so hard-ass, Art.
Ain't this just an accident?
Moran finds his eyes drifting to Ishmael's. Which are right there, waiting. Moran looks
away.

MORAN
Course it is, but a man's dead,
William. I got to write my report.
ANGLE...Ishmael and Moran, walking alone back up the wharf. The
Sheriff is worried. Finally...

MORAN
I'm not gonna see some article about an investigation, am I?
ISHMAEL (quietly)
You want me to lie?

MORAN
No, I wanna be off the damn record, that's what I want.
No answer. They keep walking.

MORAN
I mean, if there is a killer, why would you want him all alerted?
Silence. Silence. And slowly...

ISHMAEL
Let's say...someday I need some cooperation from you on this thing.

Do I get it?
And looks over. Like the guy holding all the aces.

INT. COURTROOM - DAY
Moran fidgets on the stand.

NELS (O.S.)
No sign of a struggle, you say.
SEE him now. NELS GUDMUNDSSON, attorney for Kabuo Miyamoto, stands beside his impassive client. Nels is 79, blind in his left eye, a little shaky. His body is winding down.

MORAN
Well, the coffee cup was layin' right in the <u>middle</u> of the floor, like I said. And with a fella so neat as
Carl, that did seem peculiar.
And Nels begins to walk toward him. Limping, as he comes.

NELS
As peculiar as a struggle between a 235 pound man, and an assailant strong enough to subdue him...that leaves only a <u>single</u> overturned <u>cup</u> in its wake?

HOOKS (O.S.)
Objection, asking the witness to speculate.

NELS
My gosh, Alvin, was I supposed to object every time you did that?
A real. Friendly smile.
JUDGE (wearily)
That's quite enough horseplay,
Nels, why don't you act your age?

NELS
If I did that Your Honor, I'd be dead.
Some gentle laughter. Judge Fielding doesn't even bother to look annoyed.

JUDGE
Any more homely loveable tricks, and you'll be worse than that.
Proceed, gentlemen.

HOOKS
There's an objection, Your H...

JUDGE
And it's overruled, answer the question. If you can recall it.

MORAN
Maybe the assailant straightened the cabin. And forgot the cup.

NELS
Right. In the middle. Of the floor.

MORAN
Maybe.
Nels nods to himself, as if considering that. So that the jury will do the same.

NELS
I think you testified <u>all</u> the lights were on. Cabin, mast, net lights, picking lights...

MORAN
Yessir, there'd been real heavy fog.

NELS
And yet you started the engine right up. With all those lights drawing all night, the batteries had that much charge. Did that strike you odd?

MORAN
Didn't think about it at the time.
So no, it didn't strike me odd.

NELS
Does it now?

MORAN
A little. Yes. You have to wonder.

NELS
You have to wonder.
And lets that sit. Scratches his neck.

NELS
You found three batteries, you say. A D-6 and D-8 in the well.
And a spare D-8 on the cabin floor.
Correct?

MORAN
It is.

NELS
Now I did some measuring down at the chandlery. A D-6 is one inch wider than a D-8.
It would be too large for the deceased's well.

MORAN
He's done some on-the-spot refit- ting. You could see the side flange was banged away
to make room for the D-6.

NELS
But he had a spare D-6, you said.
Right there. Why not use that?

MORAN
It was dead. We had it tested.
Maybe the D-6 was the spare and he had to use it.
Ah.

NELS
Maybe he carried a spare that was too large to fit. So he'd have to bang out the flange
to squeeze it in?
No answer to that. The silence rests.

NELS
Sheriff, how many batteries and what size did you find on <u>defendant's</u> boat?

MORAN
Two D-6's. That's the kind his well was fitted for.

NELS
No spare.

MORAN
No.

NELS
So the defendant went out fishing for the night with <u>no</u> spare battery, hmmn?

MORAN
Apparently.

NELS
I'm curious. The D-6 that was refitted into the deceased's well.
Was it exactly the same brand and model as defendant's?
A beat.

MORAN
I believe so.

NELS

Now you've testified that the deceased was a heavy man, and hard to bring out of the net.
Stops. Thinking.

NELS
Is it possible his head struck the transom, or the stern gunnel, or the net roller, as you were bringing him in?

MORAN
I don't think so.

NELS
You don't. _Think_ so.

MORAN
He was heavy, but we were real careful. But I don't remember him hitting anything, anywhere.

NELS
You don't. _Remember_.
And clears his throat.

NELS
Operating this winch you'd rarely operated before, doing this awkward job of bringing in a drowned man of
235 pounds...is it _possible_. Possible that he struck his head _after_ death. Possible?

MORAN
Possible. But not darn likely.
NELS (turns to jury)
No further questions.
And limps back to the defendant's table. Where Kabuo Miyamoto sits watching him.

INT. COURTROOM - LATER
Horace Whaley, the county coroner, folds his stork-like limbs uncomfortably. Searching for the appearance of ease.

HOOKS
...so when the sheriff returned, you showed him the injury to the deceased's head.

WHALEY
He said, 'Could it be somebody hit him?' And I said, 'You want to play Sherlock Holmes, here?'
Shakes his head, with a wry, disgusted smile.

HOOKS
Did you say more?

WHALEY
I said that if I was playing Sherlock
Holmes...I'd maybe look for a...
Japanese person. With a bloody gun- butt. A right-handed fella, to be precise.

HOOKS
And why. Is that?
Slight shrug.

WHALEY
Well, I was a doctor in the Jap theater, in the war. I saw those kendo wounds, <u>many</u>
times. Looked exactly like this one.

HOOKS
Could you tell me what 'kendo' is?

WHALEY
Japanese stick-fighting. They're trained as kids, y'know. To kill with sticks.
And the prosecutor's eyes drift to the defendant. So that the jury's will do the same.
HOLD on Kabuo's regal bearing. His neutral mask.

HOOKS (O.S.)
No further questions.

EXT. STRAWBERRY FIELDS - DAWN
Mist of early light. Two dark figures, little more than silhouettes, measuring each other
with their lethal bokken staffs.
We may think of Luke Skywalker and Darth Vader, for one is a full- grown man. The
other, eight years old. Dialogue plays in subtitled JAPANESE...

ZENHICHI
Hips, stomach, <u>cut</u>. Stomach muscles tighten as stroke advances...
And STRIKES a fearsome blow, which the child REPELS with startling proficiency.
We can see ZENHICHI's stony face, now. If he is impressed by his son, he does not
show it.

ZENHICHI
Elbow soft, or there is no follow- through. You cut your bokken off from the power of
your body, unl...
WHAP! WHAP! WHAP! The boy LASHES fiercely, the man parrying each stroke with
blinding ease.

ZENHICHI

Hips sink more. Less weight on the heels, so tha...

CRASH! The father has sent a blow in mid-word, FLINGING the child like a doll. The boy BOUNCES up, snatching his bokken into ready position.

ZENHICHI (very quiet)

Zenshin. Is constant awareness.

Of dang...

WHAP! The child has unleashed a blow at the left side of his father's HEAD. It has been blocked. The staffs rest against each other, just above Zenhichi's ear. There is no anger in either warrior. That we can see.

ZENHICHI

Elbow soft. A little better.

LATER...father and son sit on the ground, eating a small meal.

The sun has risen, angling light across the undulating fields.

They are alone in beauty. A long silence. Dialogue in subtitled

JAPANESE...
ZENHICHI

You can be good with the bokken.

If you begin to concentrate.

Eyes on his food. As if alone, as if speaking to himself. The boy darting glances, unseen, at his father's profile.

ZENHICHI

You must choose now, Kabuo. At eight years. If you want this.

KABUO (boldly)

I want it.

The father keeps eating. Never turns.

ZENHICHI

Then speak quietly. So you may be heard.

INT. COURTROOM - MORNING

Whaley stares down the end of his needle-nose. The air of disdain of a man playing chess with an unworthy opponent.

NELS (O.S.)

So this...foam you found in the lungs. How does it get there?

WHALEY

As I testified. It occurs when water, mucus and air are mixed by respiration. I believe I said that.

NELS (slightly confused)

But a drowned person can't breathe.

WHALEY

Of course not. The foam means that he went <u>in</u> breathing.
Ah.

WHALEY
That's <u>why</u> the autopsy report identifies <u>drowning</u> as the cause of death.

NELS
Meaning that he wasn't murdered first, say on the deck of the boat, and then thrown overboard.

WHALEY
Well...

NELS
Your report says death by <u>drowning</u>, which means he went into the water alive and breathing. And the report is accurate...?
WHALEY (bristles)
Of <u>course</u> it's accurate, but...

NELS
Of course, it is. Now as to the head injury. You say made by an object narrow and flat. That is your <u>inference</u>, correct?
WHALEY (really pissed)
It's my <u>job</u> to infer, that's what coroners do. You get hit with a crowbar, or a ball-peen hammer, or fall off a motorcycle, the injuries look different, that's my area of expertise.
Nels nods. He can be quiet now. The witness distracted from volunteering the opinions Nels did not wish for.

NELS
In your motorcycle example. Those injuries are produced by the head being propelled <u>against</u> an object.
Rather than the reverse, yes?

WHALEY
Obviously.

NELS
Can you tell whether an object moved against the head, or the other way around? Or would both look the same.

WHALEY
The same.

NELS
So if his head struck something narrow and flat, the gunnel of a boat, a net roller, a fairlead, could that have...

WHALEY
If the head was moving fast enough, but I don't see how it could be.

NELS
Is it possible?

WHALEY
Sure, anything's poss...

NELS
Is it fair to say that you do not know for <u>certain</u> which it was.

WHALEY
I already said that, b...

NELS
<u>And</u> that you can't say for <u>certain</u> whether the head injury was sustained before or <u>after</u> death?
Whaley thinks.

WHALEY
For certain, no.

NELS
But you are <u>certain</u> that he died by drowning.

WHALEY
For the third time, yes.
Nels nods. Whaley is beyond frustrated.

WHALEY
Can I say something, here?

NELS
Yes, you can tell me about the minor cut you found on the deceased's right hand. The report says 'recent origin'. How recent? As much as 24 hours before death?

WHALEY
Absolutely not. Probably one or two hours. Four at the most.
A pause.

NELS
Are you absol...

WHALEY

<u>Yes</u>, I'm sure.
Nels nods. Silence.

NELS
Thank you, Horace. No more questions.
Horace wants to say more. Doesn't immediately move.

JUDGE
We'll take our luncheon recess.
Reconvene at...2 o'clock sharp.
The gavel CRACKS onto the block. Judge Fielding stands to leave, and the BAILIFF begins to usher the jury from its box. Abel
Martinson, the deputy, stands near as Kabuo rises. As he puts his hand gently on Kabuo's arm, the defendant turns smoothly...
...to face a woman. Standing at the rail. And beneath the courtroom buzz...

KABUO
How are the kids?
The voice so colloquially American, we are taken back. Having envisioned Kabuo as a silent Samurai.

HATSUE
They need their father.
The look holds. Abel increasingly uneasy.

KABUO
Well. Just a few more days.
ABEL (coughs)
Look, Art's gonna want me t...
KABUO (ignoring him)
You look beautiful.
Abel grasps his arm.

HATSUE
I look terrible. Don't sit so straight like Tojo's soldier. The jury will be afraid of you.
He thinks about that. Abel tugs him.

KABUO
Okay, I'll hide under the table from now on. That make you happy?
And for the first time. He smiles. And seems suddenly very
American indeed. She stares back, her heart in her eyes. Abel tugs harder, but he can't budge the defendant.

KABUO
I'm not going until you smile.
But she doesn't. So his fades. One last look. And he lets Abel lead him away.

HOLD on her. Watching him go.

EXT. MANZANAR INTERNMENT CAMP - NIGHT
Stars above a desert. Wind gusts. PAN barbed wire, rows of dark barracks blurred by swirling dust, to...
...a fragile tar paper structure, its 'walls' rippling pre- cariously. And inside, to see that it is...

INT. BUDDHIST CHAPEL - NIGHT
...a makeshift sanctuary. Candles, offerings of fruit. A young
COUPLE together before a Buddhist PRIEST. Kabuo and Hatsue.
Becoming one.

INT. BARRACKS - LATER
A cramped, ramshackle room. Dust blowing through gaps in the flimsy beams. Kerosene light. FUJIKO IMADA hangs the last of the woolen army blankets to divide the room in half, as her four youngest DAUGHTERS watch. We PUSH THROUGH the blankets to the other side, to see...
...the newlyweds. Standing at a window in their wedding clothes.
Kissing. Slow and full. Until she whispers into his ear...

HATSUE
They'll hear everything.
And her young husband turns. Speaks to the curtain.
KABUO (loud)
There must be <u>something</u> good on the radio!
She giggles. His hands trace her body.
KABUO (louder)
Wouldn't some <u>music</u> be nice?
And in a moment. The MUSIC begins. Glenn Miller. A song that sent our boys off to war. And our young American prisoners...
...begin to undress each other. Her slender fingers find the buttons of his shirt, deftly undoing it, as he kisses her face.
He unclasps her dress. And as it falls from her shoulders, falls to the floor, we PUSH INTO her eyes, and...
INTERCUT her MEMORY of...
...a beach. Two 10-year-old CHILDREN floating on the water.
Clinging to a wooden box, with a glass bottom for fish-watching.
The girl is Asian. The boy is not.

HATSUE
Ishmael. See the yellow one?
And the boy wriggles around, leans over the box, as if seeking a better view. And KISSES the girl. Full on her startled mouth.
BACK TO...the newlyweds. On their cot now. Close together. Naked and hungry for each other.

KABUO (loud)
Can the music be <u>louder</u>, please?
We can't hear so good in here!
The girl laughs soundlessly. And as the music BLARES, he has slid his body above
hers. A whisper...

KABUO
Have you ever done this?
A whisper back, sure and strong...

HATSUE
Never. You're my only.
And as he enters her. As she holds him close with all her strength. Her lips breathe into
his ear...

HATSUE
...so right.

INT. COURTROOM - DAY
Hatsue watching her husband disappear through a door. RACK FOCUS to see across
the way. A man stares at her.

ISHMAEL (V.O.)
Course, we grew up together.

INT. IMADA PARLOR - DAY
Hatsue at 12, sits with an OLD WOMAN who guides her silently, exquisitely, through
the ritual of the tea ceremony.

ISHMAEL (V.O.)
Her mom had this Mrs. Shigemura come on Wednesdays. Teach her how to be Japanese.
The woman turns the cup in her hands. One-quarter turn. Bows slightly, as she presents
the tea.

ISHMAEL (V.O.)
Dances, calligraphy. Doing her hair.
How to sit without moving...

EXT. HOLLOW CEDAR - DAY
Hatsue and Ishmael, both 12, are sprawled on the ground, sheltered in the hollowed-out
base of a cedar tree. They watch the rain as it pummels the woods around them. She is
speaking, carefully, thoughtfully. He listens with complete attention.

ISHMAEL (V.O.)
She would tell me stories of this woman and her lessons. As if complaining, or at least
ex- plaining her world...

He shifts his position, his body brushing against hers, which makes him reflexively pull away. She seems not to notice.

ISHMAEL (V.O.)
But I always fantasized. The lessons were for me.

INT. BEDROOM - DAY
Hatsue sits at a bedroom mirror. Mrs. Shigemura watching analytically, as Hatsue weaves her hair into a thick plait.

MRS. SHIGEMURA
No. You must never look at a man directly. This is <u>part</u> of grace.
The girl smiles a small sour smile. Speaks quietly...

HATSUE
I don't think the boys on this island. Are impressed. By grace.
The old woman studies her without irritation.

MRS. SHIGEMURA
Hakujin know nothing of life, Hatsue.
Apparently, the girl has heard this before.

MRS. SHIGEMURA
This is why they fear death. Because life here is separate from Being.
The girl takes a long pin. Begins carefully to fasten her hair.
Breaking eye contact with the mirror.

MRS. SHIGEMURA
It is why they have no soul.
Is the girl even listening? The old woman's voice never rises.
Remains patient.

MRS. SHIGEMURA
Life embraces death, includes it.
This truth brings tranquility. You must see yourself...

HATSUE
...as a leaf. On a great tree.
No irony in the girl's voice. No disrespect. The old woman reads the young face in the mirror.

MRS. SHIGEMURA
The pin. Could be better placed.

INT. SAN PIEDRO REVIEW - DAY

CLOSE on 12-year-old Ishmael. Neutral eyes. Eating an apple. A horrific CLANGING surrounds us. The clash of metal on metal.

ISHMAEL (V.O.)
My lessons came from my father. They were different. Or seemed so, at the time.
See ARTHUR CHAMBERS now, at the printing press, an enormous lime green contraption, with rollers and conveyor pulleys in a cast- iron housing. The shrieking of metal and gears recalls an ancient locomotive.

ISHMAEL (V.O.)
He operated the Review alone, with an integrity and passion for principle that made him a figure of respect. If slightly larger than life.
Arthur is a large, rugged man, with round gun-metal rimmed spectacles and garters on his shirtsleeves. He wears the soft, perpetual smile of an Oxford Don, as he gracefully ducks in and out of the machine, inspecting plates and printing cylinders.

ISHMAEL (V.O.)
He never spoke of wanting me to succeed him. And, in truth, it was the last job on earth I thought I'd ever want.
The boy rises now. Sets his apple carefully aside. And under his father's supervision, takes his place operating the press. His arms inches from the fearful clatter of the rollers.

ISHMAEL (V.O.)
When I was five, he casually mentioned that if his sleeve got caught in the press, he'd be instantly popped open like a child's balloon, and splattered across the walls.
Watch Ishmael running the monster, coolly, efficiently, with complete concentration.

ISHMAEL (V.O.)
Even his bones would disappear, to be discovered later on the floor, as strips of white confetti.
Arthur turns away, lest his son feel a lack of confidence. Picks up the boy's apple. A crisp BITE.

ISHMAEL (V.O.)
Which, of course, made me certain that life would have no meaning until I could run that teakettle.

EXT. MAIN STREET, AMITY HARBOR - SUNSET
Arthur and Ishmael, now 17, strolling Main Street in the midst of what seems a festive carnival.

ISHMAEL (V.O.)
He was, for better or worse, the only God in my life. I guess it's our nature to resent those we know we can never measure up to...
They are passing modest parade floats, booths with food and games.

A genial crowd of farmers, fishermen, families, both races heedlessly mingling. A community. Arthur unselfconsciously slips his arm over the shoulder of his tall son.

ISHMAEL (V.O.)
...which keeps us from accepting the warmth. The way we should.
Up ahead, a crowd has gathered at the steps of the courthouse.
Something's up.

ISHMAEL (V.O.)
Every summer, after harvest, the
Strawberry Festival was Dad's favor- ite story to cover. Good news was his preference. Making him an oddity among journalists.
As we approach, we see a ceremony begin at the top of the courthouse steps.

ISHMAEL (V.O.)
Highlight was crowning the Strawberry
Princess. Always a Japanese girl, sort of an unwitting virgin sacrifice to the concept of racial harmony.
We are there now. Arthur pulling down the same box camera Ishmael would use years later. Focusing up at the MAYOR, as he places the crown on the radiant young girl...

ISHMAEL (V.O.)
Senior Year. It was Hatsue.
And as the applause ripples through the crowd. As the Strawberry
Princess acknowledges her subjects, her eye falls on...
...Ishmael. She drops him a wink. And a special wave.

ISHMAEL (V.O.)
She winked at me. In public.
Which was unusual.

EXT. SOUTH BEACH - DAY
Two 14-year-olds alone on a beach. Digging for clams in the mud.

ISHMAEL (V.O.)
I had kissed her once, when we were ten. Looking at fish through a glass-bottomed box. It was just an impulse, and no big deal.
Ishmael pulls back from the deep hole, to make room for Hatsue to reach down. We can see her fingers explore the shell of the dug-in geoduck clam.

HATSUE
He's still got a good grip. We need to dig more.

ISHMAEL (V.O.)
At school, she kept mostly to the

Japanese kids, and sort of ignored me. As if all of our times alone together...in the hollow cedar, everywhere...were a secret.

They are digging now, together. Carefully.

ISHMAEL (V.O.)
I told myself that was good. That it made our friendship special. And didn't mean she was ashamed of it.

Necessarily.

HATSUE
Easy. Slow is best.

Gently, she begins to dislodge the clam from its lair.

ISHMAEL (V.O.)
I thought about her. Sometimes, all the time. I knew I was unhappy.

But I knew if I told her...

She lifts it clear. And as she admires its size and roughness with her fingertips. As she washes it in the shallows. He watches her movements.

ISHMAEL (V.O.)
It might be a mistake. I could never correct.

ISHMAEL (quietly)
I like you.

The words make her turn. Not startled, exactly. Alerted. But neutral, without affect.

ISHMAEL
Do you know what I mean, Hatsue?

I've always liked you.

There is no answer. He leans slightly closer, and she looks down. This is the moment. Afraid and driven, he moves slowly to her face. And puts his mouth against hers. She lets him and, encouraged, he pushes harder, making Hatsue...

...lose her balance, and planting a hand beneath the water to support herself, eyes closed too tightly, she kisses Ishmael for a long moment, before...

...leaping up, snatching her clam pail and running AWAY down the beach like a deer. He stands slowly. To watch her go.

ISHMAEL (V.O.)
I knew in my heart that we would love each other forever.

His face is slack and unsmiling, but he is helpless with happiness. Contemplating this truth.

ISHMAEL (V.O.)
The way she kissed me. She knew it, too.

EXT. IMADA FARM - DUSK
Ishmael crouching at the edge of the farm, in near-darkness.

ISHMAEL (V.O.)
She avoided me for a week.
Across the distance, the screen door opens, light slips across the porch. Hatsue appears with a wicker basket, to take the laundry from the line.

ISHMAEL (V.O.)
So this way, I could see her without...bothering anyone.
He watches, rapt, as she unpins and folds the clothes, clenching the clothespins in her teeth. Then reeling the line again, elegant hand over elegant hand...

ISHMAEL (V.O.)
I was certain everything would work out.
She corrals the long sweep of her hair, knotting it deftly, before heading inside.

ISHMAEL (V.O.)
And frightened.

EXT. STRAWBERRY FIELDS - DAY
Children working fields in sunlight. Kneeling in the rows. Hatsue with a half-dozen Japanese girls, her hair loose, her face lightly sheened with sweat. She works with efficiency and grace, filling her flat.
Three rows away. Ishmael watches. The fear not far beneath the surface of his quiet, dark features.

ISHMAEL (V.O.)
By two weeks, I knew I had made the defining mistake of my life.
Hatsue's gaze drifts slightly in this direction, and Ishmael looks
DOWN rapidly at his work. Cheeks burning, certain she is watching.
Which she is not.

ISHMAEL (V.O.)
I'd ruined everything.
LATER...end of day. The young pickers turning in their flats as a gentle rain begins.
Hatsue counts her money, slips it into her pocket, and...
...runs lightly off, into the growing rain. Ishmael sees.
Stricken to his soul with longing. And indecision.

EXT. CEDAR GROVE - DAY
Hatsue, drenched, alone with her thoughts in the protection of the hollow cedar. The rain is driving now, and she glances up.
At something we don't see. And watches it. Finally...

HATSUE
You followed me, huh?

PULL BACK to see him. Rain pelting off his poor soaked form. She is waiting for an answer. So...

ISHMAEL
Sorry. It sort of...happened, I just...I followed you. I'm sorry.
She pulls her hair behind her ears. A movement which stretches her body.

HATSUE
I'm all wet.
She starts refastening her hair now, looking away. He comes inside, crouches as respectfully far from her as he can. Which is close. He watches her, watches her, and...

ISHMAEL
I'm sorry I kissed you on the beach.
No reaction. As if she hasn't heard. Now his heart is beating straight through his chest.

ISHMAEL
Let's just forget about it.
Forget it happened.
She picks up her damp straw hat. And, eyes down, tracing a finger around its brim...

HATSUE
Don't be sorry. I'm not sorry about it.
His heart bursts within him. And he struggles to keep it from his face. Even though she isn't watching.

ISHMAEL
Me neither.
She turns her face to him, and offers a small smile. It is genuine, and therefore dazzling to the boy. She lies back on the ground. Her eyes so unafraid and direct.

HATSUE
Do you think this is wrong?
He swallows. Staring at her lying there so comfortably.

ISHMAEL (V.O.)
The best part was that there was a
'this'. To debate the wrongness of.

ISHMAEL
Your friends would. Your dad would kill me with a machete.

HATSUE
We're Japanese, not Mexican, Ishmael.
He'll slice you up with a ceremonial sword.
Ah. Better. They are both grinning now.

HATSUE
My mom. Would be the problem.

ISHMAEL
Why? We're only talking.
Her eyes flicker. The synapse that a woman can offer a man.
HATSUE (softly)
Sure.
And touches his hand. With her fingertips. The barest whisper...

HATSUE
I can't hear you.
Thus invited, he leans down over Hatsue. Kisses her mouth with all the tenderness in
him. This time, her eyes close gently. And her body arches slightly, into his.

ISHMAEL (V.O.)
We kissed for half an hour, that first time. And I knew there would never be another
day like it.
Rain POUNDING now. A curtain of water, sealing them from the world.

ISHMAEL (V.O.)
No matter how long I lived.

INT. COURTROOM - DAY
CLOSE on Ishmael, once more in the row of reporters. Absently kneading the stump of
his amputated arm. The way some men drum their fingers.

HOOKS (O.S.)
...you were acquainted with the defendant <u>and</u> his family.
ETTA HEINE is a linebacker in a dress. Stout and German and wary.
She is 57, and pulls her hem down tight below her knees.

ETTA
Him and his folks and two brothers and two sisters worked our land.
Lived in a picker's cabin at first.

HOOKS
So the defendant knew the deceased, your son, even then.

ETTA
They fished t'gether. Went to school.
Carl Junior treated him like a white person. Like any friend.
Said not with pride, but regret.

HOOKS

But the dispute began. With the father, yes?

INT. HEINE FARMHOUSE - DAY
Etta twenty years younger, watches stoically from the parlor window, as her husband
CARL SENIOR strools the strawberry fields with Kabuo's father Zenhichi. Carl is a
huge rawboned man, and puffs a pipe as Zenhichi stops, sweeps his arms this way and
that.
Etta knows trouble when she sees it.

INT. KITCHEN - LATER
Etta pours her husband's coffee. It is very quiet.

ETTA
Don't sell, Carl. You'll regret it.

CARL SR.
Only seven acres, and the worst seven, at that. They're decent folks. They got five
hunnerd to put down _now_.

ETTA
Don't go wavin' new church clothes at me. We're not such paupers as sell to Japs, are
we? For what, a pouch of fancy pipe tobacco?
She walks about the kitchen with her arms folded. Too upset to be still.

CARL SR.
They work hard, live clean, don't spend nothin'. Even kind to the
Indjuns. People is people, comes down to it.
Etta turns sharply. Glares at the big man. He just blinks blandly, puffs his pipe. She can
see this ship has sailed.

ETTA
You wear the pants, doncha? Go ahead, sell our land to a Jap and see what comes of it.

INT. COURTROOM - DAY
Hooks pacing, slow and calm. This part needs to be clear.

HOOKS
But back in '34, Japanese-born could not _own_ land. So...?

ETTA
Carl held it _for_ 'em. Called it a lease. They make payments every
June and December...

HOOKS
Why? If they could never take title.

ETTA
Their kids was born here. So when the oldest, that one there, was twenty...last payment gets made, and he could own it.
She folds her hands. Looks Kabuo square in the eye.

ETTA
But they missed their last two payments. So that was that.

INT. FARMHOUSE KITCHEN - DAY
Carl Sr. and Zenhichi sit at the table. There is coffee. But it is untouched. Etta watches by the stove.

ETTA (V.O.)
March 1942, orders came down. Japs had eight days before the Army was gonna cart 'em off.
Carl lights his pipe. Compassion in his broad weathered face.
CARL SR. (softly)
Eight days. It ain't right.

ZENHICHI
We must leave everything. If you like, you can work our fields, sell berries, keep the money. Otherwise, they just rot.

ETTA (V.O.)
Japs are shrewd. Offer berries he can't use. Soften us up about those two payments still to come.
And sure enough, Zenhichi produces a neat stack of bills. Puts them on the table.

ZENHICHI
Today, I have $120 toward next paym...

CARL SR.
Absolutely not, Zenhichi. I'm not gonna take your savings at a time like this.
The small man spreads the bills out. On the table.

ZENHICHI
Please, you take. Then, I send more from where I'm going. If not enough, you still have seven acres strawber...

ETTA
Thought you was <u>givin'</u> us those.
And everything. Stops.

ETTA
Didn't you come in here givin' them away? Now you want $130, <u>after</u> our labor and fertilizer. Is <u>that</u> what you come here hopin' on?

Zenhichi keeps his anger within. His face is stone.

ETTA (V.O.)
I spit on him, and he's pretending it didn't happen that way. How could anyone trust people like that?

ETTA
You want more coffee?

ZENHICHI
No, thank you. Take money, please.
But Carl is staring at his wife. She stares right back. Carl turns, slides the money toward Zenhichi.

CARL SR.
Etta's been rude to you, and I apologize for that. You keep this money, and those payments will work out fine. Somewhere down the road.

INT. PARLOR - TWILIGHT
Silence. Palpable. Two figures sit at opposite ends of this darkening room, each under a lamp. Carl Sr. is reading the paper.
His face is stone. Etta at a small writing desk strewn with bills and ledgers. Her face is angry.
A screen door opens. Slams shut. Big footfalls coming. No one looks up.

CARL JR.
Look at this!
He stands in the doorway. A bamboo fishing road in his giant hand.

CARL JR.
Kabuo loaned it to me. Til he gets back.
And his parents stare back him.

CARL JR.
It's great for sea-run cutthroat.
The ferrules are smooth, silk wrapped.

ETTA
Take that back. And do it now.
The big young face is stunned, hurt.

CARL JR.
I told Kabuo I'd take ca...

ETTA
Those Japs owe us. I don't want nothin' confusing that.

The boy looks to his father. Who says nothing.

ETTA
I said now, boy. Supper's in forty minutes.
Crestfallen, defeated, the boy backs away. Hear his footfalls.
The screen door SLAM hard.
And Carl Sr. looks at his wife. No sound, until...

CARL SR.
We ain't right together.
The words are flat and straight. Etta stoic.

CARL SR.
You and me. We just ain't right.

INT. COURTROOM - DAY
Hooks settles back. His butt on the edge of the prosecutor's table. The soul of patience
and clarity.

HOOKS
You said neither of the last two payments were made. But your husband told defendant's
father that he could pay them...what, 'down the road'.
And straight back...

ETTA
Road ended October 1944, when my husband passed away.
She nods. That's all there was to it.

ETTA
I sold all the land to our neighbor, Ole Jurgensen. Got a fair price, this time. <u>And</u>...
Straightens her spine. To deliver the clincher...

ETTA
Sent <u>all</u> their equity back to those
Japs down in California. Which I didn't <u>have</u> to do. Specially since my boy was out in
the Pacific, gettin' shot at by Japs at the time.
Hooks pauses. As if drinking this in.

HOOKS
Now defendant's father had also died by that point. Where was the defendant? When
you sent his family their equity.

ETTA
In the war. Europe, I believe.
They could hardly send him to the
Pacific, could they?

Kabuo watching the woman. Eyes as hard as her own.

HOOKS
And when he came home. Did he write you about this? Or phone, perhaps.

ETTA
Just showed up at my door, big as life and twice as mean. Wanted to talk to my son.

INT. ETTA'S APARTMENT, AMITY HARBOR - DAY
Kabuo stands at the open door. No one is inviting him inside.

ETTA
He's over the ocean, fighting the
Japs. They're just about licked.
KABUO (quietly)
Just about.
And there it sits.

ETTA
When Mr. Heine passed away, I couldn't farm the place myself, could I? You're gonna
have to talk to Ole abou...

KABUO
I just did. He didn't know we were one payment away. You didn't tell him Mr. Heine
promised my fath...

ETTA
I was s'posed to <u>tell</u> him there's some illegal contract muddling things up? You folks
didn't make your pay- ments. In America, bank comes in and repossesses your land. I
didn't do anything wrong.
Kabuo stands. Calm, unblinking.

KABUO
Nothing illegal. Wrong is a different mat...

ETTA
Get out of here.

KABUO
You sold our land out from under us, Mrs. Heine. You took advantage of the fact that
we were gone. You...
SLAMM. The door has closed in his face. And Kabuo stands there.
As if deciding.
Whether to break it down.

INT. COURTROOM - DAY

Hooks standing at the jury box now. Looking at them, as he asks...

HOOKS
What do you mean by 'dirty looks'?

ETTA
Well. Every time I see him in town or somewhere, he's starin' at me with these narrow eyes.
Givin' me his mean face.

HOOKS
When your son came back from the war, what did he say about all this?

ETTA
That he'd keep an eye on Miyamoto.
Watch out for him.

HOOKS
Did he see some <u>danger</u> from defen...

NELS
Objection. Asking witness to speculate about deceased's state of mind.

HOOKS
All right. What did your son <u>say</u> to that effect?
She looks up. As if trying to recall.

ETTA
He said he wished Kabuo would forget about his seven acres, and stop lookin' at us cross-eyed.
Hooks stares at the jury. Holds the moment.

HOOKS
Your witness.
And goes slowly back to his seat. Nels waits until his opponent is seated. Then, rises.

NELS
Just three questions. The Miyamoto family bought your seven acres for

$4500?
ETTA
Tried to. Defaulted on their payments.

NELS
Second question. What did Ole
Jurgensen pay you per acre?

ETTA
A thousand.

NELS
So that makes what would have been
$4500 into $7000, doesn't it? If you sent the equity back, you had a profit of $2500.

ETTA
Is that your third question?

NELS
It is.

ETTA
You done your math right.
The old man wears a thin, cold smile.

NELS
You, too. No further questions.
HOLD on Kabuo. As he watches Etta rise heavily from the box.

EXT. DEEP FOREST - FIRST LIGHT
Mist of moments before dawn. As tendrils part, there is enough light to see...
...eyes. They are Asian. They are razor-keen. PULL BACK to reveal...
...Kabuo alone in G.I. gear and helmet. Rifle up high, sweat on his face, moving soundlessly, turning in a circle as he goes, until...
...he stops. A heartbeat of silence. Then...
...the BLAST of automatic tracer TEARS through trees, as he WHIRLS and RETURNS FIRE in a single motion, until...
Silence.
His heart is pounding. He waits. Waits. Weapon at the ready, he pushes THROUGH the dense foliage to see...
...the 15-year-old German SOLDIER, splayed on the forest floor, his chest torn and bloodied. Kabuo's gaze LOCKS with the boy's. The young soldier's empty left hand reaches out in a a plea, and as
Kabuo steps forward, the boy's right hand comes suddenly...
...INTO view, metal GLINTING in motion, as Kabuo...
...BLOWS the boy AWAY with staccato rifle BURSTS that JUMP the already-lifeless body like an electric jolt. And falling from the kid's hand, not a pistol, but...

...ID TAGS.
No expression on Kabuo's face. None at all. He moves on.

INT. COURTROOM - DAY

OLE JURGENSEN wobbles slightly in the witness box, hands resting on the cane planted unsteadily between his frail legs. His eyes leak water, his beard is wispy and unkempt.

HOOKS
Were those his <u>exact</u> words?
OLE (shaky)
He say Mrs. Heine robbed him.
Mr. Heine never woulda let no such ting like that hap...

HOOKS
Robbed. He was angry.

OLE
Oh, yeh. He said someday he would get his land back.
Hooks nodding. Nodding.

HOOKS
Mr. Jurgensen. Did he offer to <u>buy</u> the seven acres from you?

OLE
Oh, yeh. But this is nine year ago, I had my healt, I wasn't wantin' to sell.

HOOKS
And then your stroke came this summer. And you put your property on the market, I believe you said
September 7. Which, remember, is <u>eight</u> days before Carl Heine died.
And who comes Spetember 7, wanting to buy?

OLE
Carl Heine came.
Hooks pauses. Lets that sink in.

HOOKS
But Carl was a fisherman. And successful at it.

OLE
He said he didn't want that life no more. He'd been saving to buy a farm. He was sorry I got sick.
But pretty excited to get back his father's place.
The old man's head bobs. Recalling.

OLE
Liesel and me. Was happy for him.
Hooks smiles. As if he would be happy, too. Anyone would be.

HOOKS
And later, that <u>same</u> day. Only <u>eight</u> days before Carl Heine died.
Did another prospective buyer appear?

EXT. FARMHOUSE PORCH - DAY
Ole sits in a wicker chair at a wicker table. His wife LIESEL is setting out cold drinks.
But their visitor stands rigid, disbelieving.

LIESEL
I'm sorry to tell you, we took his earnest money, he shook Ole's hand.
Come November, he'll sell his boat, and take over the farm.
Kabuo is thunderstruck.

KABUO
But your sign...

OLE
We din't have no time to take it down.
He just come ten o'clock.
Kabuo nods. His voice is soft, but his eyes are steel.

KABUO
It's my fault. I should have come earlier.
He looks so odd, perhaps he's ill. Liesel looks concerned.

OLE
If you want t'buy them seven acres. Carl Heine's the only fella can sell 'em.

INT. COURTROOM - EVENING
The witness box is empty. The snow outside the windows is falling in darkness. And
Judge Lew Fielding is leaning his frame toward the jurors...

JUDGE
I apologize for keeping you folks from your families in a storm like this. I do hope you'll
be reasonably comfortable in the hotel tonight. And one more thing...
He smiles softly.

JUDGE
This Court takes judicial notice of the fact that tomorrow is the 13th anniversary of the
attack on Pearl
Harbor.
Slight pause. To make sure they are listening.

JUDGE
Which has <u>no</u> relationship to this trial. Which is why I mention it.
Gavel CRACKS down.

JUDGE
10 o'clock tomorrow, folks. Stay warm.

INT. COURTHOUSE CORRIDOR - MINUTES LATER
Hatsue walks briskly down the crowded hallway, her eyes searching the benches lining the corridor ahead. Her view obscured by the crowd hurrying to fight the storm. Suddenly...
...she stops. Because there. On a bench. Sits Ishmael. Next to him, a round Japanese-American baby boy of 11 months. Before him, squat the boy's sisters, eight and four. All are watching
Ishmael...
...manipulating a COIN. It rolls across his knuckles and back again, with amazing dexterity. Then, he snatches it into his palm.
Holds up his fist. All little eyes are glued. The fist...
...opens. It is EMPTY. There are GASPS.

ISHMAEL
Know where it is?
They don't.

ISHMAEL
It's in my other hand.
The four-year-old LAUGHS. Her big sister socks her. And Mom steps in. The man looks up, with the sweetest smile.

ISHMAEL
Your mother went to the bathroom.
She said I could show them a trick.

FOUR-YEAR-OLD
HE DOESN'T <u>HAVE</u> A OTHER HAND!
Hatsue is not smiling. Nor is she angry. Even awkward comes to her in a graceful way. She scoops up her son.

HATSUE
Thank you for your help.
(to the girls)
Let's go find obaasan.
And without even glancing at him, she heads off at a brisk pace.
The girls following. The four-year-old turning back to wave once.
And then they are gone.

INT. JAIL - NIGHT
Kabuo stands outside the open steel door of his tiny cell, as Abel

Martinson clumsily unfastens the manacles. A cot, a toilet without a seat, a bare bulb hanging from a wire. No windows to the outside world. Only the small barred one in the cell door. As the manacles fall away...

...Abel removes two objects from his pocket.

ABEL
This is from Nels, I can't see the harm. Don't tell Art, okay?
Hands him two CANDY BARS. A Snickers. And a Baby Ruth. Kabuo looks at them...
In spite of himself. Kabuo smiles. Remembering...

INT. JAIL - DAY
Kabuo sits in jailhouse overalls on the edge of his cot. Motion- less. On a private journey of the mind. The door CLANGS open...

MORAN
This here is Nels Gudmundsson, he's your attorney.
Kabuo looks over. That flat, unsmiling gaze. The old man has a folded chessboard and a Havana cigar box under his arm. Their eyes lock, as if the Sheriff weren't even here. And Moran leaves, closing the door with respectful quiet.
Nels doesn't smile, doesn't speak. Opens the chessboard on the cot. Opens the cigar box filled with chess pieces, two cigars, a Snickers and a Baby Ruth. He puts the candy bars by Kabuo's pillow, a silent gift. Begins to set up the chessboard.

KABUO
What makes you think I play?

NELS
Your daddy played. I asked, down at the Japanese Community Center.
You smoke cigars?
And offers one up, rough and black.

KABUO
I'm not sure. I better check down at the Center.
Kabuo smiles only with his eyes. Nels nods, maybe you better.
Lights his own cigar. Puts the matches and the other cigar at
Kabuo's side.

NELS
White or black?

KABUO
You mean, do I like to take the offensive? Or hang back and wait.
That seems answer enough for Nels. He turns the board around to where he has white, and makes the first move.

NELS

Nice. When two fellas understand each other.
Kabuo picks up the cigar. STRIKES a match.

.... white. Kabuo moves a black bishop. Nels' eyes
shoot around the table. He reaches and KNOCKS OVER Kabuo's black king. Kabuo
blinks, studies the board silently. Then smiles.
He unwraps the Snickers bar. Breaks it in half. Hands one piece across to his lawyer.

SERIES OF ANGLES...
RAPID CUTS, different days, Nels in different suits, chess pieces in different positions,
each time Nels reaching to topple Kabuo's king. The last time...
Kabuo has to study the board for a beat. Shakes his head.

KABUO
You must think I like losing.

NELS
I think you like learning.
And leans his old bones back against the hard wall.

NELS
Me, too. That's why I come.
Pulls out two cigars. Kabuo looks at them.

NELS
Bet there's a few things you could teach me. Kendo, for one.

KABUO
Sure. I could take a fishing gaff and split your head open.
Right above your left ear.
No smile. Steady gaze.

KABUO
You wouldn't even see it move.

NELS
You're wonderin'...how come I never ask. If you did it.
Hands one cigar. Across the chessboard.

NELS
Now, you've told me you killed four men. In Germany. So I know you are the kind of
man who can kill. When there's a reason.
KABUO (very quiet)
Guess I am.
Takes the cigar. Rolls it between his thumb and forefinger.

NELS
You feel guilty. That you took their lives. That's in your eyes.
STRIKES a match.
NELS (softly)
Jury sees what I see. More often than not.
Reaches stiffly. Kabuo bends toward him. Accepts the flame.
Takes a puff.

NELS
Prosecutor thinks. What was your reason? To kill Carl Heine.
Kabuo says not a word.

NELS
Well, there is the land itself.
Raise your children where you were raised. Sleep with your wife at night, 'stead of bein'
alone on the sea.
Brings the match to his own cigar. Careful. Expert.

NELS
There's fairness and honor. You were cheated by that old bitch.
Boy, she is something.
KABUO (simply)
She's not alone.
Worlds within those words.
NELS (a murmur)
None of us are.
And in those.

NELS
And prejudice, like you say. Your people locked in a concentration camp. You go off
to fight for our country's freedom. Come back to this.
Shakes his head.

NELS
But Mr. Hooks has missed the <u>one</u> reason. One reason. You coulda done it.
A flicker. Behind the defendant's eyes.

NELS
I read you Etta Heine's deposition.
So I could watch your mind. Like I do when you move your rook, or when
I move mine.
A smile now. Very kind. Very sad.

NELS
And you weren't thinking about her.
Or about land. Or about you.

No, you weren't. And in the gentlest voice...

NELS
No, someone cheats you, you can rise above that. You're a family man. You put them ahead of you, hmmn?
He sighs. But...

NELS
Wasn't you she dishonored.
And the old watering eyes are rock steady now.

NELS
Your father was a strong and tireless man. Honest to a fault.
Kind, and humble as well...
There is a silence. And then...
KABUO (real quiet)
Nice. When two fellas. Understand each other.
They let that sit.

NELS
Now this jury is gonna be lookin' at the evidence with one eye.
And at you with the oth...

KABUO
Mr. Gudmundsson, we <u>know</u> what that jury is looking at.
He won't let hs eyes lie to this man.

NELS
Your father needs you. To return to your family.
Silence.

NELS
So every time you think about showing that jury strength. Or honor or composure. Or dignity.

KABUO
I should show them an American?
Nels sees the rage. It breaks his heart. It makes him feel old and helpless.

NELS
Show them an innocent man.
What he stares at now. Is a neutral mask. As powerful and opaque as the voice is quiet.

KABUO
Shame you couldn't play chess with my dad, sir. He'd kick your ass.

INT. ISHMAEL'S APARTMENT - NIGHT
Through glass, snow is tumbling in endless cascades, the world dwarfed by a descending heaven. A sound, a strange soft CLICK.
PAN across...
...the small, well-kept bachelor apartment. Neat stacks of books on the floor, catching the overflow of shelves crammed full.
Someone likes to read. Another soft CLICK. To...
...the kitchen now, along the floor. An awkward high-top SHOE, its buckled straps above elastic LACES that fasten across the instep.
The shoe steps on a crude wooden PEDAL. And we hear another CLICK.
PAN up along a vertical strip of mesh WIRE to...
...a plywood CONTRAPTION, held by a partially closed drawer. A piece of spring steel holding a set of NAIL CLIPPERS.
Ishmael inserts his pinkie carefully. CLICK. Finishes clipping the fingernails of his only hand. And looks out. At the magic of white.

EXT. HOLLOW CEDAR - DAY
Safe within their haven, the 18-year-olds kiss and hold each other urgently. Their tongues exploring each other's mouth, her legs open beneath her skirt, pressing her body up against him.

ISHMAEL (V.O.)
I gave her all of my soul to love.
I knew someday we would live in
France. Italy. Somewhere. Far from the things that upset her.
ANGLE...later, they lie so quietly. Her head nestled in the crook of his arm, he gently plays with her hair. Her face so still, so thoughtful and grave.
ISHMAEL (a murmur)
You don't have to be so tragic, you know.
Ah. Her dark eyes flicker.
HATSUE (dry)
Kind of magical, the way you know how to comfort a girl.
She cuts the irony by sending her fingertips to stroke his.

HATSUE
I can just feel my spirits soar.

ISHMAEL
Well, I don't do it for just anybody.
And kisses her head. But her eyes still stare off into the tangle of her worries. He draws a breath...

ISHMAEL
There can't be any wrong in this, Ha...

HATSUE

I lie to my parents every day.
And every night.
His light tone against the fear...

ISHMAEL
Well. Since I never told your folks, I guess I'm lying to 'em, too. But you don't hear me complaining about it.
She winds her fingers with his. Loyalty against her doubt.
Very soft with...

HATSUE
I'm in awe. Of your strength.

INT. SCHOOL BUS - DAY
Hatsue sits with the Japanese kids. Ishmael with his friends. The bus filled with stone-faced teenagers listening to the DRIVER, who brandishes his newspaper at the Japanese side of the bus...

DRIVER
...not <u>just</u> Pearl, they're attackin' <u>all</u> over the Pacific, the whole <u>fleet</u>'s destroyed. The FBI's in
Seattle right now...
And pauses. His eyes moving from one Japanese face to the next.
Are you listening?

DRIVER
...arresting Jap traitors, the spies and everything. There'll be a blackout tonight, so keep your radios off. So the Japs don't pick up no signals. You get the message?
Stares them down. Until, from across the bus...

ISHMAEL (O.S.)
Hey, Mr. Lamberson, over here!
The driver's eyes snap around. The tall boy is waiting.

ISHMAEL
I have a radio, too. Don't you want to be sure <u>I</u> got the message?
Ishmael sees the anger. He's not afraid of it.

ISHMAEL
Just checking.

INT. SAN PIEDRO REVIEW - LATE NIGHT
The horrid CLANGING of the great rattletrap press, Arthur Chambers ducking nimbly among the rollers.

ISHMAEL (V.O.)

It was a special edition, an extra.
My father wrote, 'These people are our neighbors, they have sent their sons to the United States Army...'
Print flying onto paper as it rolls through the green metal gauntlet.

ISHMAEL (V.O.)
'They are no more an enemy than our fellow islanders of German or
Italian descent.'
Belary-eyed Ishmael, pulling finished copies from the bin. As he stacks them for delivery, he reads aloud, above the CLASH of metal...
ISHMAEL (sleepy and loud)

LET US SO LIVE THAT, WHEN IT IS OVER,
WE CAN LOOK EACH OTHER IN THE EYE.
AND KNOW WE HAVE ACTED HONORABLY.
Big yawn. It's really late. He turns, and sees...
...his father. Staring at him.

ISHMAEL (V.O.)
I guess courage never inspires the young. Until the danger of it bites their butt.

EXT. WOODS - TWILIGHT
They walk slowly up the path. An arm around each other's waist, their bodies brushing as they go...

HATSUE
My father can't get our money from the bank. We have a few dol...

ISHMAEL
It'll be over soon. I can get you money.
She stops. By a weathered fence, covered in vines. It's growing dark.

HATSUE
It's not going to get better, okay?
She sighs. He moves close, looks so grave.

HATSUE
They arrested Mr. Shirazaki, because his farm is near a navy transmitter. And his family can't leave their house.
What can he say.

ISHMAEL
It's just Pearl Harbor. People are a little crazy, right n...

HATSUE

Look at my face. It's the face of the people who did that. My father hardly speaks English. We're in bad trouble, you have to see that.
He reaches. Touches this face that he loves with all his heart.
Forces up a smile.

ISHMAEL
Maybe we can fix your eyes.
She leans up. CROSSES her eyes in a goofy expression. Then kisses his mouth. When she pulls back...

ISHMAEL
Don't let this hurt us, okay?
Whatever happens.
And she studies this boy. Knowing more than he can ever understand. And chooses to whisper...

HATSUE
It won't. You'll see.

INT. IMADA FARMHOUSE - NIGHT
Hatsue and her older daughter are setting the farmhouse table, as snow drifts down beyond the window. Plates and flatware. Glasses and napkins. Slowly, in silence, as if a ritual bonding mother and daughter. She glances to the next room...
...her mother Fujiko plays with the babies. Her father HISAO reads the paper. Smoking his pipe.
And Hatsue is motionless for a moment. Watching him.

INT. IMADA FARMHOUSE - DAY
CLOSE on Hatsue at 18, staring with silent anger greater than her fear.
HISAO (O.S. shaky)
We are loyal.
PULL BACK to see the room. Hatsue and her sisters side by side, staring at the table. On it rests a shotgun, four boxes of shells, a ceremonial sword. An FBI AGENT, a small man in a dark suit, is tagging each item. He wears a light, perpetual, insincere smile.

FUJIKO
Everyone on the island has these things.
Fujiko at her husband's side. She is quietly indignant. He is frightened.
AGENT (overly casual)
Well, they'll hold this stuff for a little bit, then ship it back to you. It's nothing to worry about.
And walks over to the tansu, a chest of drawers, and begins to remove items...

AGENT
You folks have been real polite, and we'll be outta your hair in just a second...
...a silk kimono with gold brocaded sash...

AGENT

That's very nice. From the old country, it appears. Very high class.
And lays it on another table. Next to a bamboo flute, a stack of shakuhachi sheet music.

AGENT

These are real nice things.
They'll take special care of 'em.
Hisao sees his wife's sudden alarm. And, as respectfully as he can manage...

HISAO

The flute is precious. The kimono, the music. Must you take th...

AGENT

...oh yeh, any old country stuff, we have to take.
And sees on the sofa, an open album. Strolls over.

FUJIKO

This is only my daughter's scrapbook. For her memories.
So he picks it up. Doesn't see Hatsue stiffen with repulsion, as he wanders, thumbing
through it, toward the hallway...
AGENT (calling out)
Wilson? Don't go pawing through the underwear!
And chuckles. He knows they appreciate a joke. It means there's nothing to be afraid of.
Stops turning pages now. Looks up, his eyes moving until they find Hatsue.

AGENT

Strawberry Princess, huh? You musta been flattered by that.
Looks just like y...
The soft slamming of a screen door. Another AGENT, large and shambling in his too-
small suit, is carrying a crate. And a telling look.
AGENT #2 (quiet triumph)
Dynamite. Twenty-four sticks.
And the crate BANGS onto the table. Just beside the kimono. Lifts out two sticks and
holds them high. Proof.

HISAO

You must believe. This for tree stumps. For clearing land.
The small man's smile fades now. First time. And his eyes fix
Hisao before he speaks. As if reading his mind.

AGENT

Maybe. Maybe. But this is still bad, y'see.
Fujiko slips her hand into her husband's. To give him strength.

AGENT

It's illegal contraband, you were s'posed to turn this stuff in.
We, uh...
Slight shrug.

AGENT
We gotta arrest you. Have to take you to Seattle.
Fujiko's breath catches. One of the daughters whimpers. The silence hangs thick and frightening. The bigger agent unhooks a pair of handcuffs from his belt, but...

AGENT
Naw, you don't need those. Mister
Eee-ma-da-san here is a class act, a real gentleman.
The younger girls are crying now, clinging to their sisters. The agent regrets this.

FUJIKO
Please, reconsider. He has done no bad th...

AGENT
Well, nobody knows that yet, do they? So, best for an honest man to clear his name for godd and all.
Ain't that right?

AGENT
Only a few questions in Seattle, okay? Few questions, few answers, the whole thing is over.
He puts his hand on Hisao's arm. Not roughly, but much firmer than the ease of his voice...

AGENT
Simple as that.

INT. FARMHOUSE KITCHEN - NIGHT
Eight pages of a letter, carefully written in Kanji characters, folded neatly on a table.

FUJIKO (O.S.)
Why do I read you this distres- sing letter? From your father.
From this hakujin...work camp, it is called. In Montana.
PULL BACK to see mother and five daughters around the table. Even the youngest girls somber, attentive. As if they have aged these past few weeks.

FUJIKO
Because you need to know the darkness. In the hearts of the hakuj...
HATSUE (blurts)
Not all of them.
The silent wake of her outburst, her interruption, lingers. Her mother studies her.

FUJIKO
The whites are enslaved by their egos,
Hatsue. Each believes his aloneness is everything. We seek union wi...

HATSUE
...the ones seeking union with the
Greater Life bombed Pearl Harbor.
They are <u>not</u> humble. I am <u>not</u> part of them, I'm part of <u>here</u>.
Her voice so loud, so insistent. Her sisters are afraid for her.
To have shown such disrespect. They look down at their hands. Or away, as if not hearing.
FUJIKO (quietly, slowly)
I see this. This lack of purity is a mist around your soul. I see it every day, it haunts your face in unguarded moments.
The room is still as the grave. The mother's eyes burn silently.

FUJIKO
I see it in your eagerness to leave here. And walk the woods.
In the afternoon.
What does she know? Hatsue's heart pounding. And to her surprise, her mother's voice softens...

FUJIKO
If you lose your true self, Hatsue.
True self...
The stern warning, the unrelenting judgement, has become a plea.

FUJIKO
There is no way back.

INT. ISHMAEL'S KITCHEN - NIGHT
Ishmael washing his supper plate. His fork and knife. His coffee mug. His skillet. Hard labor with one hand. And as he works, he looks at...
...the window above his sink. Darkness and moonlit snow. And his own reflection. CLOSE on his face in the glass, and MATCH DISSOLVE to...

INT. SAN PIEDRO REVIEW - NIGHT
...Arthur Chambers. Weary. Worn behind the smile of knowing ease, as he sips coffee from a mug of his own.
His boy sits across from him in the silent press room. Feet up, reading their paper. Its headline, ISLAND JAPANESE ACCEPT ARMY

MANDATE TO MOVE.
ISHMAEL
See, you bring it on yourself.

23 ladies honored by the PTA, you single out three names. And they're all Japanese.
That isn't journalism.
ARTHUR (quietly)
Because...?
Ishmael has heard this gently prodding word all his life. He sighs.

ISHMAEL
Because journalism. Is just the facts.

ARTHUR
Which facts? You can't print them all. Journalism is balance.
Finding the facts folks need to know.
The boy looks dryly at his father. SLAPS the page with the back of his hand.

ISHMAEL
Hence. The letters.
Arthur closes his eyes. Recites from memory...

ARTHUR
'Seems like you're favoring the Japs,
Art. Writin' all about their patriotism and loyalty with nothin'
'bout the treachery.'
A smile in the voice. A sad one.

ARTHUR
'Your newspaper is an insult to all white Americans. Please cancel my subscription and
send refund.'
Now the smile is on his face. Even sadder.

ARTHUR
The calls are better. 'Jap lovers get their balls cut off and stuffed down their...'
(shrugs)
Missed the rest. Hanging up will do that.
Silence. Two men. Watching each other.

ARTHUR
We lost the Price-Rite ads. And
Lottie Opsvig's shop, and Larsen's
Lumberyard and the Anacortes Cafe.
And 30 percent of our subscribers.
A deeper silence.

ISHMAEL
Integrity is expensive stuff, huh?

ARTHUR

Valuable things. Sometimes are.
Toasts his son. With coffee.

ARTHUR
But. I've got the answer.
A wink. A swallow of Joe.

ARTHUR
Print four pages. Instead of eight.

EXT. HOLLOW CEDAR - DUSK
They lie so close. Their bodies touching, not moving. Their faces inches apart, so that every word is a murmur...

HATSUE
You're like me. You've learned to be devious.
He's never seen her this fragile, this scared. He knows he has to be strong for her.

ISHMAEL
It's not devious, it's what we have to do. You're leaving tomorrow...
He unties her hair. So gently. Tries to keep his smile calm, steady...

ISHMAEL
You write to my house, and put
Kenny Yamashita's name on the return address. It's no big deal.
He brings his face to her hair. Kisses it.

ISHMAEL
You smell like cedar.
Her eyes are wide. They move over his face. A murmured...

HATSUE
So do you. It's your smell I'll miss as much as anything.
He looks in her eyes. And words come from his heart, before he can stop them...

ISHMAEL
Let's get married, okay?
Her eyes fill with tears. Are they from happiness?

ISHMAEL
I want to marry you. Is that okay?
Her face so still. One tear falls, and he kisses it.
ISHMAEL (a whisper)
Just say yes.

No answer. Not knowing what to say, she winds an arm behind his head, and brings him nearer. His mouth opens into hers, with more force, more of his heart, than he has ever given. Deep and tender.
His hands reach beneath her dress...
...peel her panties down her thighs...

ISHMAEL (V.O.)
When something that means your whole life. Is the last time ever...
And suddenly, he is OVER her, drawing her legs up around him...

ISHMAEL (V.O.)
God should tell you. Or it's not fair.
Her head tilts back, her eyes squeeze closed. And as he enters her...
ISHMAEL (whispers)
Please say yes...
...her hands GRASP his upper arms. And push away.
HATSUE (softly)
No.
And he blinks. As if waking from a dream. Everything has stopped.
Her face is strong and yet overflowing with regret.

HATSUE
No. No. It isn't right.
So he draws away. Stunned, uncomprehending. Watching with blank eyes, as she stares up at him. Then, with dignity and tenderness, he helps her dress, his eyes awkwardly away from hers...

ISHMAEL
It felt right to me. It felt like getting married.
She draws her legs up. Kneeling now, putting her hands on his face...
But no words come. No words. Until...

HATSUE
I'll write you.
And KISSES him fiercely, and BOLTS up before he can grab her,
RUNNING off like a deer, while he...
...kneels. His mouth open. Like a silent scream.

EXT. AMITY HARBOR FERRY - MORNING
An army truck pulls up behind several others in cold morning air.
Hesitantly, looking in all directions, Fujiko, Hatsue, and her four sisters climb from the truck, to see...

ISHMAEL (V.O.)
On Monday, March 30, 1942, the
United States Army graciously transported the Imada women to the docks.

...a ferry, the KEHLOKEN, stands waiting. Soldiers are dis- tributing tags for luggage and coats. The evacuees, mostly women, stand in the cold, trying to smile bravely for each other. And lined against the railing...

ISHMAEL (V.O.)
Lifelong neighbors came to watch.
Curiosity masked as kindness...
...a cluster of white islanders gawking as their Japanese neighbors file toward the ferry. A middle-aged woman waves to Fujiko, who casts her eyes down, refusing to acknowledge the greeting. And just as they reach the gangway...
...Hatsue sees Ishmael, who stands at an unobtrusive distance, among a group of students. She pauses. Her eyes hold his for a heartbeat...

ISHMAEL (V.O.)
...with some exceptions.
The wisp of a smile. And she is gone.

EXT. IMADA FRONT PORCH - NIGHT
Hatsue comes alone onto the white-blanketed porch. Snow is no longer falling. She takes out a cigarette, lights it impassively.
The mannerisms make her seem fully American, despite the porcelain impenetrability of her Asian exterior. She closes her eyes, and...
...draws deep on the smoke. The act seems to cause her pain. When the eyes open, they are frightened, unguarded. Nowhere to turn.
The next puff looks desperate, and she FLIPS the cigarette out onto the snow. Jams her hands in the pockets of her parka, stamps her feet against the cold, the helplessness. And looks out...
...strawberry fields, endless and white, shimmering in filtered moonlight, become...

EXT. MANZANAR INTERNMENT CAMP - NIGHT
...a moonlit DESERT. PAN the barbed wire, the distant barracks, the desolation. Come to...
...two women walking alone. The younger one glancing at her mother as they go. Fujiko's eyes unreadable, stare implacably ahead.
The barracks, everything, in distance behind them.

HATSUE
You think we're far enough away now?
No sarcasm in the voice. She lets the words carry her irony.
Her mother stops. Looks at her so directly, so strong. Even her tough-minded daughter flinches slightly.

HATSUE
Mom, whatever this is, they don't keep <u>war</u> secrets this carefully.
Fujiko thinks that over. Nods.

FUJIKO

Secrets are hard to keep.

She goes over to a large, flat rock. Sits down. Pulls two sheets of paper from her coat.
And waits. As her daughter comes and crouches at her feet. Fujiko clears her throat.

FUJIKO

This letter. Was opened.
By mistake.
And watches. As the shard of fear penetrates her daughter's mask.
Silence. Then...
FUJIKO (reads)
'My love. I still go to our cedar tree in the afternoons every day. I shut my eyes, waiting.'
Hatsue has turned to stone. To ice. Wind blows.
FUJIKO (reads)
'I smell your smell. And I dream of you. And I ache for you to come home. So I can
hold you and feel you near.'
Fujiko scans the page silently. Turns to the second...
FUJIKO (reads)
'After all these years that we've been together, I find you're a part of me. Without you,
I have nothing. All my love, forever...'
And looks up. Her eyes calm, quiet.

FUJIKO

The neighborhood boy. Who taught you to swim?
The look holds. And holds.

HATSUE

You shouldn't have opened that.
It was mi...
FUJIKO (so quiet)
How deceitful of me.
Anger only at the edges. Like finely-honed steel.

FUJIKO

How can I ever hope. For your forgiveness.
The wind swirls a cloud of dust between them. They seem not to notice.

FUJIKO

I have written this letter to the boy's parents...
She pulls out a single page. Hands it down to her daughter.
Hatsue's eyes move quickly over the words.

FUJIKO

Attraction is no crime, certainly among children. The dishonor lies in the concealment.
From your families.
Watches her daughter reading. And quietly...

FUJIKO
I know that you know this. I know you have suffered. Even if the hakujin could not.
Silence. Hatsue's eyes cast down. She folds the page.

FUJIKO
There will be no further letters.
No contact of any k...
And stops. Because Hatsue is TEARING the page in two. She looks up. Into her mother's shock.

HATSUE
One more letter. I will write it. You may read it, and send it for me.
Her mother's anger fades. Into interest.

HATSUE
I deceived more than you. I deceived this sweet boy. And myself. It was never love.
Never love. The mother's face changes. There is understanding, acceptance. Even pride.

HATSUE
I will work hard. To earn your forgiveness.
A sigh. A sadness deep, beyond her years.

HATSUE
I can never hope for his.

INT. BARRACKS - NIGHT
Mother and daughter enter their crude quarters. They find Hatsue's sisters sitting on the wooden floor, watching...
...a team of young MEN, working with tools and pieces of lumber.
One is building shelves, two others, a chest of drawers. Their leader kneels tacking scraps of tin over the knotholes on the floor. One girl beams at her mother...

SUMIKO
These boys are buildings us a mansion!
The leader grins and rises. Bows slightly to Fujiko. He is, of course...

KABUO
I'm Kabuo Miyamoto, Mrs. Imada.
The woman smiles. Bows slightly in return.

FUJIKO
We are in your debt, Miyamoto-san.
How are your parents, your family...?

KABUO

My father is sick with the camp food. The rest of us are fine.
Don't speak of dept, please, we just want to help.
And glances. To the eldest daughter. In the doorway.

KABUO
Hi, Hatsue, remember me?
She looks back, without expression. There is much on her mind.
His smile is handsome, easy.

KABUO
I was a senior when you were a junior. But I've seen you around.
She tosses her hair free of the parka. Gathers it in her hands.
Saying only...

HATSUE
Hello.
Can't win a smile, but he doesn't seem to mind.

KABUO
Nice to see you.

EXT. APARTMENT HOUSE REAR PORCH - NIGHT
Ishmael steps from the building onto the rear porch. He draws from his coat a black
CIGAR. Box of matches. The cigar goes into his mouth. With amazing dexterity...
...he slips a single match from the box, turns his face to the wall, and still palming the
box, STRIKES a match on the buckle of his belt, bringing it smoothly to the cigar for a
few critical puffs before the match dies. He turns toward...
...the fields. Stretching treeless, endless, seemingly to the horizon. Bathed in filtered
moonlight, they become...

EXT. TARAWA ATOLL - NIGHT
...the shimmering Pacific. We are with Ishmael in an LCVP landing craft, as his platoon
enters Tarawa lagoon. Bobbing past two
DESTROYERS firing in waves at the beach. Ishmael and his platoon mates watch with
adrenaline-fueled fear as amphibious tractors draw fire on the sand, one exploding in
flame.

ISHMAEL (V.O.)
Her letter reached me on the North
Island of New Zealand. So I had a month to think it over...
Men around him are shouting, cursing, jostling against each other, frightened out of
their minds, as SHELLS POUND the ocean, horrify- ingly huge and near.

ISHMAEL (V.O.)
I wrote her four times. 'I hate you with all my heart. I hate you,
Hatsue, I'll hate you always!'

Suddenly their craft runs AGROUND on the hidden reef. They are still 300 yards from shore.

ISHMAEL (V.O.)
I never sent the letters. I wanted to kill as many Japs as possible.

SQUAD LEADER
MOVE IT, MOVE IT, MOVE IT,
LET'S GO!!
The SQUAD LEADER goes over the side, Ishmael and others follow, struggling with 85 pound packs. As Ishmael hits the water, the squad leader is SHOT in the face, a man five yards from Ishmael has the top of his head BLOWN AWAY, men are DROPPING in numbers under the WITHERING BURSTS of fire, the deafening ordnance sweeping over the SHRIEKS of terror and agony, and Ishmael...
...submerges behind his pack, splashing hard, keeping its bulk ahead of him as a shield, until he can wade and swim and plunge toward shore, as hellfire CRASHES everywhere, dead bodies floating, machine-gun blasts WHIPPING the water's surface, Ishmael at...
...the shallows now, men rising to make a run at the seawall, being
CUT DOWN, Ishmael crouching in the water, watching other men draw fire, and in a moment's lull, four of them and Ishmael...
...GO for it, lungs BURSTING, pounding MADLY up the sand, one
SHOT DEAD, another SCREAMS as his knee is blown away and goes down writhing, as three men...
...MAKE IT to the wall. Gasping, puking, shivering with cold and fright. They have no gear, no weapons. One of them is Ishmael.
He looks back to...

ISHMAEL (V.O.)
Eric Bledsoe was bleeding to death.
Thirty yards away.
Bullets FLYING everywhere, CHEWING up the sand. The young man twitching, pleading...
BLEDSOE (crying)
Oh, shit, please, please help me you guys, come on, help me, fucking help me, PLEASE...!
And flat against the seawall, three men watch. Not daring to look at each other.

ISHMAEL (V.O.)
I knew nothing could save him. Hell,
I didn't have so much as a band-aid.
I also knew I was a coward. For not giving up my life to try.

EXT. SEAWALL - DAY
Ishmael and his companions have been joined by others. Sixty or so men mill in the shadow of the seawall. The beach is littered with dead marines and wounded, calling

for help. As Ishmael glances up, a SERGEANT leaps ONTO the seawall, cigarette dangling from his mouth...

SERGEANT
You <u>pussies</u> are the kinda <u>chickenshits</u> deserve to have your <u>balls</u> chewed off real <u>slow</u> when this is over!
Stands with his hands on his hips. The men below him properly mesmerized.

SERGEANT
Any man who won't follow me over this wall is a cornhole-fucker with a half-inch hard-on wh...
The words CUT OFF by the shell that RIPS THROUGH his spine, OPENING his shirt front as he PITCHES forward FLAT upon the sand.
No one looks. No one speaks. It never happened.

ISHMAEL (V.O.)
I wanted to live. And I didn't know why.

EXT. SEAWALL - NIGHT
Ishmael has a carbine now and a field machete. PULL BACK to reveal
300 MARINES all down the wall, a striking force assembled from the survivors of multiple landings.

ISHMAEL (V.O.)
Some colonel came down the beach.
Any man who didn't go over the wall at 2100 would be court-martialed, disgraced and imprisoned...
Every man lining up now, rifles at the ready.

ISHMAEL (V.O.)
The captain who followed said shot on sight.
They seem more resigned, or is it stunned numb, than terrified.
There is no interaction. Each man dealing with his own insides.
And suddenly...
...squad leaders go OVER THE WALL, the firing ERUPTS, and three hundred marines SCRAMBLE into the teeth of it, mortar and machine- gun BARRAGE lighting the sky from the row of battered palm trees,
Ishmael SPRINTING, the man next to him goes DOWN, Ishmael TURNS instinctively, and a shot...
...RIPS into his left bicep, SPINNING him OFF his feet in SLO-MO, falling to dirt as all goes...

BLACK.
INT. SHIPBOARD OPERATING ROOM - NIGHT

Ishmael feverish, writhing unconscious against the straps that hold him to a table. All around him, a hell of men and blood and doctors and limbs and shouted curses they never showed us on M.A.S.H.

ISHMAEL (V.O.)
My arm was dealt with by a pharmacist's mate, whose surgical career was four hours old.
Ishmael LURCHES, his eyes pop OPEN, wild and bleary...

ISHMAEL (V.O.)
He used a handsaw.
...seeing there, in a corner, on a pile of blood-soaked dressings...
...his left arm.

ISHMAEL (V.O.)
I dream of it, now and then.
The way my fingers curled.
Against the wall.
He blinks at it. Realizing at last that the arm is his...

ISHMAEL (V.O.)
...fucking goddam Jap <u>bitch</u>!
An ORDERLY turns at the words. Nods. As if he knows.

ISHMAEL (V.O.)
It was all I could think of to say.
His eyes squeeze shut.

ISHMAEL (V.O.)
There was nothing more to say.
For a long while.

INT. KABUO'S CELL - LATE NIGHT
CLOSE on a dark blue suit. Clean shirt. Hanging on a hook against the green wall. PAN ACROSS the bars in the cell door's tiny window. All is dark out there, and silent. Here...
...the bare bulb glows. Its light throws shadows of castles and horses across the chessboard.
Kabuo cross-legged on the floor, alone. His back erect. His eyes calm. Stare at the pieces.

EXT. WOODS - NIGHT
Kabuo at 19 sits on the earth. By a shovel. By a lantern. This place is shielded by trees. PAN across the ground to...
...his father. Slowly, reverently, placing objects into burlap sacks, beside a shallow hole in the earth. Wooden swords, hakama pants, a bokken, scrolls written with care. Dialogue plays in subtitled JAPANESE...

ZENHICHI
Your great-grandfather was a samurai, a magnificent soldier.
The father never looks at the son. Only at his work.

ZENHICHI
He killed himself. On the battlefield. At Kumamoto.
The boy knows this. Yet his entire being is focused on every word.

ZENHICHI
He went to battle with a sword.
Against rifles, mind you. Knowing what honor required.
An elegant SWORD. Its curved blade gleaming in the lantern light.

ZENHICHI
He was angry. To the point of being crazy, yes. But he knew what honor. Required.
A separate sack, just for this. Folded with respect.

ZENHICHI
Honor can require loyalty.
Revenge. Death.
It goes into the ground. With the others. He seems nearly overcome now. By some
emotion that sweeps through him. Prompting the boy to murmur...

KABUO
These are safe, father. The hakujin will never f...
ZENHICHI (quietly)
...it is the only scale...
Meaning, be still. So the boy is still.

ZENHICHI
Only scale. In which our worth.
Is weighed.
The man gazes into the hole. At his treasures.

ZENHICHI
Every life ends. And if it ends dishonored. It is as if...
And turns to his son. To complete the words.
KABUO (in English)
...we have never lived.
There is love. There is strength. There is no more to say.

INT. COURTROOM - DAY
Sheriff Moran sits in the witness box, blade-thin and fidgeting ever so slightly.
Uncomfortable in the limelight. In his hands are four pieces of ROPE.

MORAN
Well, this one here comes off
Miyamoto's boat. Matches all his others, worn equal and so on. But this one here...
Holds it up for Hooks. So the jury can see.

MORAN
...comes off third cleat from the stern, port side. And it's brand new. Unlike the rest.

HOOKS
And the next one...?

MORAN
From Carl Heine's boat. All his were like this one, three-strand manila, new condition,
braided in loops. Not bowlined like Miyamoto's.

HOOKS
And the last...?

MORAN
Found on Carl's boat, too. Starboard side, second cleat from the stern.
But it doesn't match Carl's lines.
It matches Miyamoto's. perfect.
Ah. Hooks nods. Significant.

HOOKS
So if defendant had tied up to deceased's boat. With that last one. Would those cleats
have lined up?

MORAN
You bet. And if Miyamoto there had been in a hurry to cast off, he coulda left this line
behind on Carl's boat.

HOOKS
And replaced it later with the new one. That's your inference?

MORAN
Pretty darn clear.
I see. Hooks begins to pace. Toward the jury.

HOOKS
And when you visited defendant on his boat. The evening after Carl
Heine's death. Did it seem pretty darn clear to him?

EXT. THE ISLANDER - NIGHT

Kabuo kneeling at the battery well of his boat. He is sliding a new BATTERY into place. Beside its older companion. He bolts it down. Starts his engine. He is visibly tense. As he steps onto the deck, he sees...

...two figures at the pilings. Sheriff Moran makes a cutting motion across his throat, as Abel moves to grasp the mooring line.

MORAN
Cut your engine, we're coming aboard.
Kabuo doesn't move. The tension has fled beneath the surface. His face now a mask.

KABUO
What for, Sheriff?

MORAN
We have a warrant. To search your boat.
He holds it up. Abel looks uneasy, as if expecting anything.

KABUO
Well, what are you looking f...
MORAN (calmly)
A murder weapon. We think you might be responsible for the death of Carl Heine.
Kabuo blinks. As if hearing a foreign language. Words that do not compute.

KABUO
Sheriff, if somebody killed Carl, it sure as hell wasn't me.
Moran steps from the dock ONTO the boat, Abel awkwardly following.

MORAN
Then let's get this over with, so you can get to fishin'. Now, cut yor engine.
And walks ahead into the cabin, shining his flashlight across everything. Kabuo follows, killing the engine. And in the sudden silence, Moran's beam finds...
...the still-open battery well.

MORAN
You always run with the well open?

KABUO
I was checking the cables.
Moran's light moves over the batteries.

MORAN
D-6s, huh?
And says no more. Runs his beam once more around the cabin.

MORAN
We'll come back, let's take a look at the stern.

Off he goes. Kabuo's glance goes to the open well. Then follows, noticing Abel
Martinson prowling around the bow. But in the stern,
Moran is shining his light. Third cleat. Port side.

MORAN
See you replaced a mooring line, lately. This one's new.

KABUO
Naw, I had that around for a while.

MORAN
Sure you did. Help me with this hold cover, willya?
So Kabuo slides the cover away. They peer in.

KABUO
There's nothin' to see. I need to get out there fi...

ABEL (O.S.)
Art. Looka this.
He has the fishing GAFF. Three-and-a-half feet long. Steel hook at one end. Hands it
to Moran.

ABEL
There's blood on it.

KABUO
Fish blood, I gaff fish with that.
Moran carefully examines the object.

MORAN
You gaff with the <u>hook</u> end.
Blood's on the butt. Where your hand goes.

KABUO
Sure. Blood gets all <u>over</u> your hand, Sheriff, ask any fisherman.
Moran takes out a handkerchief. Holds the gaff with it.

MORAN
Gonna have this tested. Now you go home, okay? Wait til you hear from me.
Kabuo's heart is racing.

KABUO
Sheriff, I can't afford not to fish toni...

MORAN
Look, no way I'm lettin' you out there. In a half hour you could be in Canada.

Kabuo's face has gone dead. Which makes it seem somehow fierce, almost threatening. And the sheriff is watching that.

MORAN
I'm sorry, son. But you're under arrest.

INT. COURTROOM - DAY
Moran still on the stand. The ropes are gone now. His hands interlock across his narrow thighs.

NELS (O.S.)
Now your testimony was interrupted yesterday, when that power line set fire to your mother-in-law's farmhouse...
Art looks <u>really</u> irritated.

NELS (O.S.)
How <u>is</u> your mother-in-law?

MORAN
She's alright, Nels, thanks for asking.

NELS (O.S.)
And her farmhouse...?

MORAN
The damage was considerable.
But she's insured. Thanks, again.
See Nels now. Avuncular as hell. Bemused by Moran's annoyance.

NELS
Well, just to put it back in our minds, could you repeat what you told us. About the <u>type</u> of batteries you found. One Carl's boat.
Moran sighs. Tries to be patient.

MORAN
One D-6 and one D-8 in the well.
And a dead D-8 on the deck.

NELS
Which you inferred was replaced by the D-6, which must have been a spare.

MORAN
What else could it be?

NELS
Even though a D-6 is too big, and the flange had to be banged out to squeeze it in.

(beat)
Which makes it a peculiar choice.
For a spare.

MORAN
You said that. That was your testimony.
Everybody laughs. Including Nels.
NELS (chuckling)
I guess I'm a pretty smart feller, after all. And what were the type batteries you found on defendant's boat?
MORAN (bland)
D-6s. Like I sa...

NELS
No further questions.

INT. COURTROOM - DAY
DR. STERLING WHITMAN sits in his expensive suit, a giant of a man whose towering frame ill fits the witness box. His eyes are small and blue, and carry the weight of superiority with practiced ease.

NELS (O.S.)
So the blood on the gaff was not fish blood at all. It was human, yes? Type B positive.

DR. WHITMAN
Carl Heine's type.
Nels nodding. Seemingly unconcerned by this fact.

NELS
But you can't say with any certainty that the blood was his.

DR. WHITMAN
No, but as I say, the type is rare.
Ten percent of Caucasian males.

NELS
And the blood could not have belonged to defendant. Seeing that his type is O negative.

DR. WHITMAN
That's obvious.

NELS
You scraped the dried blood from the butt of the gaff. Where a fella's hand goes. And what did you see under your microscope, besides the B positive blood and the wood scrapings...?
And the witness stops. A curious question. But Nels is waiting.

With an expectant smile.

DR. WHITMAN
Bits of blood and wood. What else would there be?

NELS
No bits of bone, no particles of scalp, no strands of hair?

DR. WHITMAN
None.

NELS
Well, if the blood got <u>onto</u> the gaff by crushing a man's skull...

DR. WHITMAN
I'm a hemotologist, sir, I was asked only t...
NELS (gently persistent)
...would that seem <u>logical</u>?

DR. WHITMAN
I don't know.

NELS
You don't.
Nels lifts the gaff off the table. Looks at it.

NELS
The coroner testified that Carl
Heine had a cut. A fresh cut.
Probably one or two hours old.
And grasps the butt end. Of the gaff.

NELS
On the palm. Of his right hand.
Walks, dragging one leg just slightly, toward the box. And holding the butt of the gaff
toward him...

NELS
With no bone or scalp or hair present. Would it be more probable that the blood came
from crushing a man's skull...

DR. WHITMAN
I'm a hemotologist, not a detective.

NELS
...or from the cut on his hand.

Which is more probable?
Whitman won't be badgered. His smile carries only a trace of coldness...

DR. WHITMAN
It is not my function. To weigh those probabilities.
Nels looks him over.

NELS
You're right.
And turns his back. Walks away.

NELS
...that's the jury's job.

INT. COURTROOM - DAY
Hooks in pin-stripe serge today. Pommaded hair, glossy wing-tips.
He is crisp.

HOOKS
Now this regiment you were training, the 442nd, this was all Nisei boys...
First Sergeant VICTOR MAPLES wears his green dress uniform, splashed with decorations. Thick and powerful, no neck, razor cut.
The eyes are alive.

MAPLES
They were Japanese-American boys, yes sir.

HOOKS
And you were generally experienced in training men for hand-to-hand combat.

MAPLES
It was my specialty, sir, I trained several thousand over the years.

HOOKS
So. Wide cross-section of men to evaluate. And the day that the defendant volunteered for this... demonstration. Did you find him eager?

MAPLES
More than eager. He was out to make a point.
Hooks finds that interesting. Begins to pace.

HOOKS
And what point. Was that.

EXT. TRAINING FIELD, CAMP SHELBY, MISSISSIPPI - DAY

The squad of Nisei recruits, one hundred young Asian faces, surround Sgt. Maples. He paces before them, holding up a wooden staff, looking in their eyes...

MAPLES
Anyone.
And Kabup steps forward. Bows slightly. Then salutes...

KABUO
SIR!
Maples stares. Hard.

MAPLES
You don't salute me, you don't call me 'sir', soldier, I'm an enlisted man.
Kabuo stares back. Blank.

MAPLES
And nobody <u>bows</u> in this man's
Army, you're in America, son.
Not Japan.

KABUO
I'm sorry, sir, force of habit.

MAPLES
No more 'sir'. That's the last of that.
Tosses Kabuo a wooden staff and a helmet. A little hard. As Kabuo slips the helmet on...

MAPLES
The exercise is avoiding thrusts.
Now, first y...
KABUO (quietly)
Ready, sergeant.
Cut off in mid-word, Maples glares back. Are you? THRUSTS sharply, but Kabuo moves just enough to slip the blow by no more than an inch. Their eyes lock. Suddenly, Maples unleashes...
...a SAVAGE series of THRUSTS at blinding SPEED, and Kabuo...
...SLIPS them all effortlessly, scarcely seeming to move. As a man might toy with a child. Maples studies the face for any trace of mockery. And sees nothing at all. STABS out, only to have Kabuo...
...SLASH Maples' staff from his grasp, with a move so quick as to be nearly invisible. Maples clearly STUNNED by the display.
KABUO (quietly)
Excuse me.
He bends, picks up Maples' staff, hands it to him. And bows.
Slightly. The sergeant is hot. He looks into the faces of this

Nisei regiment, searching for a single smirk. There is none.

MAPLES
Are you ready for some simulated combat, soldier?

KABUO
For combat. Sergeant.
And Maples LUNGES with surprising speed, to be SWEPT off his feet in a BLUR,
lying FLAT on the earth, his head PINNED to the ground by the tip of Kabuo's staff.
A hush. Kabuo withdraws his staff. Retrieves Maples'...
KABUO (just above a whisper)
Your weapon, sergeant.
And bows.

INT. COURTROOM - DAY
Maples smiling easily. Like a guy telling the story in a bar.

HOOKS
Well, what then, sergeant?

MAPLES
What else? I had the boy teach me kendo. Including...the importance of the bow.
Everyone laughs. Maples the loudest. Hooks smiles like a regular
Joe.

HOOKS
And your evaluation of the defendant? Could he kill a much larger man with a fishing
gaff?
So quickly, there would be no sign of struggle?

MAPLES
Oh, in a heartbeat.
And the smiles are gone. All around.

MAPLES
Able and willing. Like few men
I've ever seen.

INT. COURTROOM - DAY
Hooks sits against the prosecution table. His demeanor gentle, respectful. His voice soft.

HOOKS
So the plan was for your husband to fish through the prime season.
Then, in November, sell the boat.
And you would move onto the farm.

In the box, the widow sits in lovely dignity. Blonde and alabaster and modest, in her black dress of mourning.

SUSAN MARIE
That was his plan, yes.
In the press row, the boys are attentive. An angle they know they can sell. Ishmael among them, watching with neutral eyes.

ISHMAEL (V.O.)
Whatever she said, she was Hooks' star witness. The jury, especially the men, would not betray this fine lady with a not guilty verdict. How could they face her?
Hooks walks slowly toward her. As if she were a precious object, deserving of reverence.

HOOKS
Can you think back for me to the morning of September 8? The day after your husband purchased the farm. One <u>week</u> before his death.
Can you recall that morning?

SUSAN MARIE
I can.

INT. BATHROOM - DAY
A bright bathroom, filled with STEAM, filtering the sunlight. PUSH toward the opaque shower door, TOWARD the sound of rushing water.
And of breathing. THROUGH it to...
...Susan Marie and her husband. Her arms are wound about his neck.
Her legs wrapped around his body, feet locked behind the small of his back. Carl holds her high with his strong hands, so he can lick her breasts to the rhythm of the slow, slow thrusts. Her wet blonde hair is pasted across her face, and her eyes are closed.
The intensity holds us.

INT. PARLOR - MORNING
CLOSE on a paint brush. It rests across the lid of a can of wood stain. See now...
...Susan Marie kneeling by the table she is refinishing. But her hands, her body, are motionless. Her eyes stare out the window...
...across the yard. Her towering husband walks beside a smaller man. Carl is doing the talking. Kabuo's face is stone.

INT. PARLOR - LATER
Susan Marie sits quietly in a rocker, nursing her baby. Her hands tenderly stroke the feeding infant. But her eyes are attentive.
Concerned.

CARL (O.S.)
What <u>could</u> I tell him? There's my mother to think about. You know what <u>she'd</u> say?

Susan Marie knows. What Etta would say.

CARL (O.S.)
I said I'd think it over, talk with you.

SUSAN MARIE
Did he go away angry?
See Carl now, pacing his own parlor like a caged bear. Agitated in a way we could not
have expected.

CARL
He kept talkin' about those seven acres <u>belonged</u> to his father, and how <u>honorable</u> and
<u>decent</u> his father was. His meaning was pretty clear.
And I didn't much like it.

SUSAN MARIE
You had a scrap.
Nursing her baby. Calm, direct.

CARL
I couldn't...<u>talk</u> to him. Look,
Kabuo's a Jap. And I don't hate
Japs, but I don't like 'em neither.
It's hard to explain if you weren't in the war, you know?

SUSAN MARIE
He's not a Jap. You don't mean that. You and he were friends.
And Carl turns. Looks at her. A full beat.

CARL
We were kids.
He looks helpless. Frustrated. He doesn't want his anger to spill onto her.
He leaves the room. Without a word. HOLD on her.

INT. COURTROOM - DAY
Susan Marie's cornflower eyes are set. Wary.

NELS (O.S.)
So your husband said he's think it over. Encouraged Mr. Miyamoto to believe he might
sell to h...

SUSAN MARIE
I wouldn't say encouraged.

NELS (O.S.)
Well, he didn't say 'no', did he?

Didn't say no hope existed.

SUSAN MARIE
Not in those words.

NELS (O.S.)
So the defendant was encouraged to hope. Or could have been.
She thinks about this.

SUSAN MARIE
I guess so.
Nels is nodding. Nodding.

NELS
I guess you'd have to guess.
Not having been there with them.
Having to guess whether your husband's report was word for word accurate.

SUSAN MARIE
Carl never lied.

NELS
Of course not. But it was emotional. A friend's plea set against his mother's attitude.
And then. As if it had just occurred to him...

NELS
Those 'dirty looks'. Defendant ever aim one of those at you?

SUSAN MARIE
He had no reason to.

NELS
Carl ever say _he_ got one?

SUSAN MARIE
I can't speak for him.

NELS
You can speak for what he _said_.
Just like you did for Mr. Hooks...

HOOKS (O.S.)
Objection, badgering the wi...
CLICK. All the lights in the courtroom go OUT. A loud murmur. A
FLICKER of light. Then, they go OUT again.

The crowd BUZZES, laughs, the gavel RAPS. The lights come ON. A collective sound of relief. The gavel AGAIN. Finally, silence.

NELS
Sorry about that, Mrs. Heine.
Shall I repeat the ques...

SUSAN MARIE
Carl said he didn't like Kabuo much anymore.
A silence. A deep one.

NELS
The question is more about the <u>defendant's</u> attitu...

SUSAN MARIE
That's all he said.
She arches her throat.

SUSAN MARIE
And we can't ask him anymore.

INT. ISHMAEL'S DESOTO, CENTER VALLEY - TWILIGHT
Ishmael driving an aged DeSoto through the blanketed strawberry fields of Center Valley.

ISHMAEL (V.O.)
My father had bought the DeSoto fifteen years before. Driving it reminded me of him. Which I considered a neutral fact...
He turns the wheel, using a cherry wood knob, specially mounted for his convenience.

ISHMAEL (V.O.)
Actually, it was pleasant.
Following the curve, fields are pure white to the horizon.

ISHMAEL (V.O.)
Snow made all the fields into one.
The notion that one man might kill another for a small patch, made no sense.
Up ahead, a Willys station wagon has run into a ditch. A middle aged Japanese man is working at a rear wheel with a shovel.

ISHMAEL (V.O.)
But I knew such things occurred.
Having been to war and all.
The man is Hisao Imada, and we can now see his eldest daughter working with a shovel behind the car. Ishmael pulls up behind them. And gets out.
He crunches over to where Hisao works...

ISHMAEL
May I give you folks a lift?
Hatsue has come around the car now, pulling her snowflaked hair from her eyes.

ISHMAEL (V.O.)
I didn't look at her. I thought that would be best.
Her eyes on Ishmael's profile, Hatsue goes to her father's side.
Murmurs to him in Japanese. WHen he answers, she turns to face
Ishmael...

HATSUE
My father is grateful for your kindness. But he will free his car, shortly.
Ishmael smiles softly. This car isn't going anywhere. He goes to
Hatsue, reaching gently for her shovel.

ISHMAEL
Okay, I'll help.

INT. DESOTO, SOUTH BEACH DRIVE - TWILIGHT
Ishmael drives with Hisao beside him.

ISHMAEL
I know it's caused you trouble.
But don't you think the snow is beautiful, coming down?
His eyes flick to Hatsue in the rearview mirror. She stares out the side window,
concentrating on the world. Two strands of wet hair pasted against her cheek.

HISAO
Yes, <u>very</u> beautiful.
Suddenly, her eyes SNAP to meet Ishmael's in the mirror. His dart away. Hers hold.

HATSUE
This trial is unfair. You should write about that in your newspaper.
He keeps driving. And he keeps his eyes on the road.
ISHMAEL (calmly)
What should I say?

HATSUE
Just that. This trial is <u>wrong</u>, they are calling a good man a killer.
It is only about prejudice, and that is unfair.
He thinks. As he drives. Hisao Imada silent beside him.

ISHMAEL
We all expect the world to be fair.
As if we have some right t...

HATSUE
I don't mean everyone. Just people who can do things because they can arrest people or convict them. Or run a newspaper.
And his eyes come up. Meet hers in the mirror.

ISHMAEL
Maybe I <u>should</u> write a column.
What do you think?
She studies his face.

HATSUE
What do <u>you</u> think?
No smile. On either side.

ISHMAEL
I think people. Should be fair.
His eyes on the road now. The farmhouse seen through the drifting screen of white.

HATSUE
Will you write that?
Her voice is soft. The difference is palpable.

ISHMAEL
I might just.
His voice is kindness and friendship.

ISHMAEL (V.O.)
I was part of her life again. I was a person.

EXT. COAST GUARD LIGHTHOUSE, POINT WHITE - DUSK
A tower of reinforced concrete, rising a hundred feet above the sea. Ishmael's hand in his pocket. Trudging toward it.

INT. LIGHTHOUSE RECORDS ROOM - DUSK
Ishmael being led into a cramped room, stacked floor to ceiling with wooden crates, file cabinets, duffel bags. Our host is
LEVANT, a young Coast Guard radioman nearly six foot six, with a huge Adam's apple, and kinky black hair. He gestures around the room at all the records. Voila.

ISHMAEL
You have the night watch? On the radio.

LEVANT
Since September. Last guys got transferred.
Ishmael looks around. There is a <u>lot</u> of stuff.

ISHMAEL
And you keep the records, or contribute to 'em.

LEVANT
Shorthard the radio transmis- sions, write 'em up, file 'em in a cabinet. Nobody ever looks.
Just take up space.
Ishmael nods. Guess so.

ISHMAEL
All kinds of radio transmissions?
Fisherman in trouble, and such.
Innocent question. Random example.

LEVANT
All kinds. Make yourself at home.
And leaves. Ishmael looks at the task before him. Then, out the window. Dark now. His reflection stares back. As troubled as he is.

INT. PETERSEN'S GROCERIES - DAY
Ishmael at 24, carrying milk and crackers down the aisle of a grocery store, the empty sleeve of his mackinaw pinned up at the elbow. He turns the corner to see...
...three people in line at the register. The second is Hatsue. An infant carried at her shoulder.

ISHMAEL (V.O.)
I'd been back two months. It was the first time I'd seen her.
He joins the line. The CHECKER glances his way, then looks awkwardly down. This makes the others turn. And Hatsue's eyes.
Meet his.

HATSUE
Hello.
The voice, the face, are cool and formal. There is no anger, no unkindness. Only the absence of warmth. Ishmael nods. His face hard, stricken. His heart pounds in his throat.

ISHMAEL (V.O.)
I couldn't say anything. I just stood there, hating her.

HATSUE
I'm sorry about your arm. Kabuo and
I. Are very sor...

ISHMAEL
The Japs did it.

No one knows where to look. Down, away, anything. But Hatsue never blinks.

ISHMAEL
They shot it off. At Tarawa.
She holds her ground, her eyes soften, somehow. Somewhere between compassion and pity. Her slender fingers stroke the baby at her shoulder.

ISHMAEL
I'm sorry, I'm sorry I said that.
All the feeling comes to his eyes. Everything he will never tell her. A murmur...

ISHMAEL
I'm sorry about everything. All of it.
He drops his milk and crackers on the counter.
And walks away.

INT. LIGHTHOUSE RECORDS ROOM - NIGHT
Ishmael sits alone. Beyond the glass, a SEARCHLIGHT sweeps the sea, the snow-covered shore. But Ishmael stares at a folder. Open in his lap.

ISHMAEL (V.O.)
September 16. At 1:42 A.M., the dead of night. The S.S. West Corona, a Greek-owned freighter, was lost.
In heavy fog.
His finger. Traces a line of the report.

ISHMAEL (V.O.)
They radioed to the lighthouse.
They would have to dogleg, bisecting
Ship Channel Bank. And Seaman Philip
Milholland wrote that down. In his report.
Ishmael closes his eyes.

ISHMAEL (V.O.)
Carl Heine drowned. In Ship
Channel Bank. And his watch stopped. At 1:47.
He looks out through the glass. As if he could watch it happen.

ISHMAEL (V.O.)
A huge freighter plowing through.
Throwing a wake big enough to fling any man overboard.
And Ishmael removes the page from the file. Slowly, he folds it into quarters. Slides it into his coat pocket.
ISHMAEL (calls out)
Seaman...?

And closes the file. Slips it back into the cabinet. Levant appears, vaguely irritated by the summons. So Ishmael smiles.
Sorry, nothing important.

ISHMAEL
How long you have this detail?

LEVANT
Me and Smoltz came on dogwatch
September 16.
Ishmael's face. Just to clarify...

ISHMAEL
You mean, early morning the 16th?

LEVANT
No, night of the 16th, morning the
17th. We replaced two guys named
Miller and Milholland.
Oh. Ishmael nods.

LEVANT
They got transferred that day.
Out to Cape Flattery.

ISHMAEL (V.O.)
Some seaman's loast report.
Stuffed in a cabinet, good as lost forever. No one knows.
Ishmael rises, stiffly. Starts to pull on his coat.

LEVANT
You get what you come for?
And Ishmael looks at the youngster. A little oddly. Admits...

ISHMAEL
Guess I'm not completely sure.
What that was.

EXT. FLETCHER'S BAY - MORNING
Ishmael at 24, crouched among trees. Above a sunlit stretch of beach.

ISHMAEL (V.O.)
I left the grocery, and wrote a letter. I apologizes from my heart.
I should never have said that word to her. I never would again.
CLOSE on his face. Eyes gazing down. At something.

ISHMAEL (V.O.)
It sat in my desk for two weeks.
Before I threw it away.
He sighs. Rises slowly.

ISHMAEL (V.O.)
I knew her car. And sometimes when I'd see it, I'd...drive that way. At a distance.
See Hatsue down on the beach. Alone, raking for steamer clams.
Her baby beside her on a blanket, beneath an umbrella.
Ishmael walks down to the sand. Crosses to where she works. And squats down. At a
respectful distance.

ISHMAEL
Can I talk to you?
She must have seen who was coming. Because the words do not startle her. Or slow her
work.

HATSUE
I'm married, Ishmael. It isn't right for us to be alone. People will t...

ISHMAEL
There's no one here, and I've <u>got</u> to talk to you.
Her back is to him. She is motionless.

ISHMAEL
Don't you owe me that?
And she turns. Her eyes go first to her sleeping child. Then she walks over, and sinks
to the sand. Just before him. Near enough to touch.
She looks in his eyes. And waits.

ISHMAEL
I'm like a dying person.
The words just came out. His eyes move over her face. His aching for her is naked,
beyond his ability to cope.

ISHMAEL
I don't sleep. I tell myself this can't go on, but it goes on anyway.
He seems at the edge of insanity. Or tears.

HATSUE
I did a terrible thing, Ishmael.
I knew what you felt. And what I didn't.
Sadness in her voice. But strength as well.

HATSUE
And I never found the courage to tell you.

His eyes swim with tears. He chokes them back, he has to.

ISHMAEL
You'll think this is crazy, but all
I want is to hold you. Just once.
And smell your hair.
She absorbs this. No sign of repulsion or anger. Her eyes seem wise. And very sad.

HATSUE
You have to hear this, I can never touch you, Ishmael. Not once, not ever. There's no half- way. As much as I know it hurts you, you have to let this go.

ISHMAEL
Look, I <u>want</u> to forget you, I do.
I think if you hold me, just this once, I can walk away and never speak to you again.
She just keeps looking at him. There is a bravery to her steady gaze. Her calm resolve.

ISHMAEL
Please? As one human being to another, just because I'm miserable and don't know where to turn. I need to be in your arms. If it's just for thirty seconds.
His pleading look holds her for a moment. In the silence...

HATSUE
I hurt for you. Whether you'll ever believe that or not.
Feeling behind her eyes. First time she lets it show.

HATSUE
I feel sick sometimes, with the guilt of what I've done to you.
And I can't make it right.
She rises slowly. Brushes the sand from her skirt.

HATSUE
To hold you would be wrong and deceitful. You're going to have to live without holding me, that is the truth of the way things are.
She takes one step back.

HATSUE
Things end. They do. Get on with your life.
And turns away. She gathers her baby in her arms. Takes her blanket, her umbrella, her rake and her pail. He watches, never moving, as she gathers her things. Gathers them as if he wasn't there. And with her back turned...

HATSUE
Get on with your life.
She walks slowly away. Her baby cries.

INT. KITCHEN - NIGHT
CLOSE on a steaming soup kettle, resting on a woodstove. A woman's hand stirs with a wooden ladle. PULL BACK to see...
HELEN CHAMBERS, slender and strong and keen. She is not yet 60. A code of fairness and self-reliance is written on the fine-boned features.

ISHMAEL (V.O.)
I drove from the lighthouse to my mother's place. I brought her some groceries.
Beyond the window, snow falls more heavily than ever. Silent.
Spellbinding.

HELEN
Your father thought that heavy snow was God's kindness. Despite the hardship, it brought us beauty...
Ishmael at the rustic table. Watching her back.

HELEN
...and reminded us. Of our place in things.
Softer. Not bitter, but regretful that...

HELEN
You don't believe in God anymore.

ISHMAEL
Agnostics don't believe or disbelieve,
Ma. We just don't pretend we know.
She begins ladling the soup into big porcelain bowls.

HELEN
We don't <u>know</u> God, we <u>feel</u> Him. You felt Him as a child. I remember.
And turns. Looks at him.

ISHMAEL
That's a long time ago. What a child feels...that's different.
She studies him silently for a moment. Then brings the bowls to the table...

HELEN
Spend the night, will you? Don't go back out into all that snow.
Sets them down.

ISHMAEL (V.O.)
I felt Milholland's report in my pocket. And wondered why I wasn't telling her. Telling someone.
What I'd found.

HELEN

You've been busy with that trial,
I suppose. Such a travesty...
She takes her seat. As he watches her.

HELEN
They only arrested that poor soul because he's Japanese.

ISHMAEL
Seattle boys think he's guilty. They say the evidence is rock solid.
She begins to eat. Eyes on her bowl.

HELEN
They're not his neighbor, like you are. He is a husband, a father, he risked his <u>life</u> for
<u>their</u> country.
The same as you.

ISHMAEL
Those aren't the facts that matter.
She looks up. Straight to his eyes.

HELEN
Well, folks are pretty cold.
And folks who believe in nothing else...they're cold, too.
No mistaking her meaning. He swallows. Uneasy as always, in the path of her
disapproval.

HELEN
I've tried to understand your unhappiness, all these years.
Having gone to war, losing your arm...
The directness of her gaze. He can't turn from that.

HELEN
But other boys came back. And pushed on. They found girls, and married, had babies...
He doesn't flinch. His voice too quiet with...

ISHMAEL
Someday I'll get lucky, too.
Too quiet to conceal the hurt. She thinks it is hurt she has caused. It changes her tone to
a plea...

HELEN
Your father fought at Belleau
Wood, it took him years to get over it. Nightmares, tears, b...

ISHMAEL
...but he found you.

Their eyes locked.

HELEN
It isn't the war, Ishmael. All those years growing up. You never had a real girl of your own.
And now he looks down. He sees that his fist is tight around the handle of his spoon.

HELEN
And I know you have it in you to love. I know that much. I wish I knew more.
His fingers open, and the spoon clatters softly on the wood.

ISHMAEL
I'll stay tonight. Thanks for asking.

INT. BEDROOM - NIGHT
Ishmael wanders through a silent room. A bed, a dresser. Work table and lamp. A room denuded of all decoration, all possessions, all sign of life.

ISHMAEL (V.O.)
I came back from the war to this room. I stayed a few months. Until my father passed.

EXT. VETERAN'S CEMETERY - DAY
Ishmael at 24, the left sleeve of his dark suit of mourning pinned at the elbow. The diggers are filling a grave in distance.
Mourners mingle, some casting glances back at Ishmael. Keeping their distance out of awkwardness rationalized as respect.
One man comes to him. MASATO NAGAISHI is aging and frail. But his voice is clear...

NAGAISHI
The Japanese people of the island are saddened by this loss. Your father was a man of great fairness and compassion for others...
He stands at a respectful distance. Ishmael clears his throat. He nods, thank you. No words to say. So the small man adds...

NAGAISHI
A friend to us. And to all people.
Silence. They are a tableau of stone. Finally...

ISHMAEL
Well...
And no more. The man takes a step back...

NAGAISHI
We know you will follow in his footsteps. And honor his legacy.
Which changes Ishmael's face. To something harder.

ISHMAEL (V.O.)
I thought it then. And often since.
A balance, he's said. Finding the facts. That folks needed to know.

INT. BEDROOM - NIGHT
Ishmael stands at an open closet. Cardboard boxes have been set aside. One has been searched for treasure. The page is in his hand. Only slightly discolored by age.

HATSUE (V.O.)
Dear Ishmael. These things are very difficult to say. I can't think of anything more painful than writing this letter.
He closes his eyes.
ISHMAEL (a murmur)
Think of reading it.

HATSUE (V.O.)
I don't love you, Ishmael. There is no more honest way to say it.
He carries the letter to the twin bed. Where he slept alone.
Thinking of her.

HATSUE (V.O.)
Whenever we were together, I knew it. I loved you and I didn't love you at the same moment.
He sinks slowly. As if beneath the letter's weight.

HATSUE (V.O.)
The last time. At the cedar tree.
I knew we could never be right together. And that soon I would have to tell you.
His eyes are dry. The letter has used up his tears long ago.

HATSUE (V.O.)
This is the last time I will write to you. I am not yours anymore.
He sets the letter on the bed beside him.

HATSUE (V.O.)
I wish you the very best. Your heart is large and you are gentle and kind. I know you will do great things in the world.
He reaches now to his inside coat pocket. Withdrawing...

HATSUE (V.O.)
I must say good-bye to you now.
Our lives will move on. The best we can.
...a page. Folded in quarters. Sets it near the letter.

ISHMAEL (V.O.)

Milholland's report was like her letter. Something no one else.
Would ever read.
He stares at them. Side by side.

ISHMAEL (V.O.)
Thing about having only one hand.
It's hard to tear pages up. And
I wasn't carrying a match.
He lies back. Across the bed.

ISHMAEL (V.O.)
So I thought of my father. The man who would have taken this report to
Judge Fielding.
Tears stand in his eyes.

ISHMAEL (V.O.)
But every reporter. Chooses his own balance. FInds the facts that matter.
Shuts the eyes. Against them. Against everything.

ISHMAEL (V.O.)
After all, the freighter was only a theory. It proved nothing at all. There were other facts.
That mattered.
We CLOSE on his face. The tightness of the muscles.

ISHMAEL (V.O.)
Tomorrow I would write a column.
About prejudice. And she would be grateful. For my large...and gentle...heart.
The eyes open, they are blank. Staring...

ISHMAEL (V.O.)
Her husband would be judged. And she would be alone.
...at the future.

ISHMAEL (V.O.)
Alone. The past looks different.

INT. COURTROOM - DAY
Hatsue Miyamoto in the witness box. Graceful, erect, her porcelain beauty accessible,
eager to cooperate. Humble.

HATSUE
Hopeful. Is the word I would use.
And Nels seems slightly surprised.

NELS
But Carl didn't say yes.

HATSUE

He didn't say no. That was Kabuo's point. Given how Carl's mother felt, Carl was <u>still</u> willing to consider selling to us. It was a good sign.
Nels considers that.

NELS

Well, in the week that followed, the week before Carl's death... did your husband pursue him?

HATSUE

No. Kabuo did not wish to beg, he respected Carl's right to reflect. He was sure Carl would do the honorable thing.
NELS (right back)
And did he?
She nods. Only once. Her eyes bright.

HATSUE

The night of the 15th, Kabuo helped
Carl at sea. With his dead battery.
Nels raises his eyebrows. To give the point its weight.

HATSUE

Right there, on the boat, they agreed. $8400 for the seven acres,
$800 down. They shook on it. Kabuo was so excited when he came home.
Nels lets that sit. And sit.

NELS

And when did you first learn.
That Carl had drowned?
The slightest pause. As if hesitant to confess...

HATSUE

One o'clock, that afternoon, from a clerk at Petersen's.
NELS (turning to Hooks)
Your witness.
And Alvin Hooks rises. Perches on the edge of the prosecutor's table. And looks at the witness with fairness and suspicion.

HOOKS

Your husband came home agitated, after his encounter with the deceased?
No impatience across her perfect features. Only earnestness will do.

HATSUE

I said 'excited'. Not agitated, he was excited in the sense of being overjoyed.

HOOKS
You were...overjoyed yourself, to hear the news?

HATSUE
Happy for him. And relieved.

HOOKS
So, then, you...and your husband... must have called friends, relatives, to tell them the amazing news. Yes?
HATSUE (calm, respectful)
No.

HOOKS
Really? Didn't call your mother, your sisters, about starting a new life. Your husband never tells his brothers that the family honor is vindicated.
Hatsue shifts in her chair. Smooths her skirt.

HATSUE
We hear how Carl...passed away.
Only a few hours later.

HOOKS
Your husband returned at, what, seven o'clock?

HATSUE
Closer to eight.

HOOKS
So, five hours. Plenty of time for a call. He was 'excited', you say.
In the sense of being 'overjoyed'.
She nods, he was.

HATSUE
We are...cautious people. You would say conservative. There would be time for celebrating with others when a paper was signed.
Hooks pouts. He allows himself that.

HOOKS
You thought the deceased might... break his promise?

HATSUE
Of course not. We're just not quick to run and boast. In case something went wrong.

HOOKS
And then, something did. Carl
Heine was found dead. With his head crushed.

She weathers that last part. As if taking no notice.

HATSUE
Yes, and then, what was there to call about? Everything was up in the air.

HOOKS
Up in the air? Was _that_ your reaction?
And he rises. Tastefully indignant.

HOOKS
I would suggest that more happened than a land sale evaporating. A man _died_, Mrs.
Miyamoto. A husband and father of small _children_ had his _skull_ bashed in!
HATSUE (quiet dignity)
If you mean to imply that we were callous about Carl's death, that is wrong and
insulting.

HOOKS
I see. Well, did you come forward to tell Sheriff Moran what you knew? The encounter
in the fog, the...dead battery, was it?
Silence.

HATSUE
We discussed that. And decided not to.

HOOKS
Why not?
She looks at him with the directness we've seen before.

HATSUE
Because the facts could be misconstrued as murder.

HOOKS
But if truth was on your side, whatever were you worried about?
Her eyes cut to Nels. He smiles, to blunt the harm she's done by looking to him for
support. Her gaze goes down now. And then...
...back up. Straight to Hooks.

HATSUE
Trials aren't only about truth,
Mr. Hooks. Even though they should be. They're about what people _believe_ is true.

HOOKS
So you hid the truth. Deliberately.

HATSUE
We were afraid. Silence seemed better. To come forward seemed like a mistake.

HOOKS

Well, it seems to me...
NELS (gently)
Objection. Mr. Hooks can give his view in his summation.

HOOKS

Doesn't it seem to <u>you</u>, Mrs.
Miyamoto, that your mistake was in being deceitful? Concealing information during the
course of a sheriff's investigation.

HATSUE

It seems human. To me.
Oh. Hooks raises his brows.

HOOKS

I suppose that you mean this <u>excuses</u> concealing the truth. Then why ahouls any of us
believe you now?
And in the silence...

HOOKS

Question withdrawn, you may step down.

HATSUE

You're implying th...

HOOKS

I said. No further questions.
Anger flashes across her eyes. Her face colors. She draws a breath...

JUDGE

That's enough, Mrs. Miyamoto, not another word. Step down, please.
She looks to Nels in her desperation and regret for making things worse. he chuckles
and waves. It's quite all right. She sits for a frozen moment. And as she rises...
The boys in the reporter's row are scribbling furiously.
All but one.

INT. COURTROOM - DAY

JOSIAH GILLANDERS folds his blunt, thick hands across his belly.
Nearly 50, sporting a walrus moustache and the watery, dull eyes of an alcoholic, he is
a man ready to make the most of his fifteen minutes of fame.

NELS (O.S.)

Thirty years fishing alone. Ever had an occasion to board another man's boat <u>except</u> in
an emergency?
Maybe to socialize or some such?

GILLANDERS (ready for this)
Never. Only boarded some fella's boat five, six times in thirty-_one_ years.
Dead engine, broken hip, only in need.

NELS (O.S.)
Now, Mister Gi...

GILLANDERS
Unwritten rule of the sea. We don't bother each other, stick to ourselves.
Ask anybody.
Nels is wandering over to the jury box.

NELS
Now if you wanted to kill a man.
Think you'd try boarding against his will, and hitting him with a fishing gaff?

GILLANDERS
It's a joke. Maneuver up to Carl's boat? Tie your lines fast? Come aboard? All against
Carl's will?
It's the stupidest suggestion I ever heard of.

NELS
I'm sorry about that. It wasn't mine in the first place.
Gentle laughter. Even some on the jury.

NELS
So the fishing gaff method wouldn't make sense?

GILLANDERS
Couldn't get on the boat. I'd just _shoot_ the feller. _Then_ tie up, throw him inta th' drink.
And skip bein' the first gill-netter in history to make a successful forced boarding.
More laughter. Hooks at his table. Simply smiles.

NELS
Now the sheriff believed that the
D-6 battery in Carl's well was
Carl's own spare. Even though it was too large f...

GILLANDERS
No sense to have _any_ at all., even the right size. It's like having an extra battery in the
trunk of your car. Nobody does.
Nobody. No way.

GILLANDERS
Boat has two batteries. Lose one you run off the other til morning.
Carl musta lost both, so Miyamoto there gave him one a his.

NELS
Course, if Carl lost both batteries, dead in the water, his radio wouldn't work. So how would he signal for help?

GILLANDERS
Compressed air horn, most likely.
Hope to God some man hears you in that fog.

NELS
All right, what if the defendant <u>heard</u>? So Carl <u>let</u> him aboard, to help. And <u>then</u> the fishing gaff?
Gillanders grins. Wide.

GILLANDERS
You mean Miyamoto followed him out there, and sucker-punched him?

NELS
Well, what if?

GILLANDERS
Now, how is Miyamoto gonna know in <u>advance</u>? That Carl loses two batteries. Must happen once ever'
20 years or so.
Another chuckle or two from the gallery.

NELS
Thank you, Mr. Gillanders. Thank you for coming down, in this cold weather.

GILLANDERS
Well, it does seem mighty warm in here. Specially for Mr. Hooks.
And looks at the prosecutor. Who rises, easily. A most polite fuck-you smile. Hooks strolls now. Slow and steady. Straight to the witness box. Rests his hands on the rail. Leans in.

HOOKS
What if the defendant follows Carl.
And pretends his <u>own</u> batteries are dead? Would Carl tie up and help?
And the smile on Gillander's face. Stops. Cold.

HOOKS
Is the word you're groping for...'yes', perha...

JUDGE (O.S.)
Alvin!

HOOKS
Rephrase. Do you agree that he might tie up to the defendant's bo...

GILLANDERS
So why's the D-6 in Carl's well?

HOOKS
Who's to say? Maybe it was just a spare, after all. Or maybe the <u>defendant</u> left it, as a potential alibi. In case somebody saw him in Ship Channel Bank.
(beat)
In case we put two and two together, knowing of the hostility.
Between the families.
Gillanders. Actually thinking about that.

HOOKS
My question is. Could Carl have tied up to help the defendant?
A beat. A cleared throat.

GILLANDERS
It <u>coulda</u> happened. And if I start to say it's doubtful, you'd probl'y say 'no further questions', right?
Once more, laughter. Enough to bring the gavel DOWN.

HOOKS
Right about that. <u>And</u> right that it 'coulda happened'.
Turns his back, walks away.

HOOKS
Thanks for your help. Hope the witness box wasn't too warm for your comfort.
All eyes follow the prosecutor, as he sits. Except for the defendant. His stare forward.
Recalling...

INT. KABUO'S CELL - NIGHT
Kabuo seated on the concrete floor of his cell, leaning back against the wall. Leaving the cot. For his guest.

NELS
But the toughest scenario. Is the one Hooks will never raise.
Kabuo watching. Quiet. Takes a breath...

KABUO
And what's that?

NELS
That you came upon Carl by accident.
Like you said. Gave him the battery.

Like you said. Asked him about the seven acres. Like you said.
The hardest. Straightest. Look.

NELS
Only. He said no.
Silence.

NELS
And something...happened. That you'd never planned. Because you're not a cold-blooded killer.
Nobody flinches. Nobody blinks.

KABUO
I'm more a hot-blooded killer, huh?
Like a soldier. Like a samurai.

NELS
You won't hear that from Hooks.
Because the charge is <u>first</u>-degree murder, which requires premeditation.
He can't change the charge.
Do you understand?

NELS
So if the jury thinks you <u>did</u> kill. but only in the heat of anger. They have to acquit.
Do you?

NELS
And you couldn't. Be. Re-tried.
Kabuo's face is stone. A warrior's mask.

KABUO
You want me to say that.

NELS
I want you. To tell the truth.
There is no kindly smile tonight. No candy bars.

KABUO
You think that <u>is</u> the truth.

NELS
I told your wife. Trials aren't always so much about actual truth.
As about what folks <u>believe</u> is true.
That's sad. And it's real.

KABUO

And what do you believe?
Nels sighs. Cocks his head just to one side.

NELS
A question first. Why do you want to know?
KABUO (straight back)
Because you're my friend.
The old man thinks about that. Studies his client.

NELS
I believe you are a good man. Who belongs with his family.
And then the feeling comes. To the watery eyes.

NELS
And I believe. You didn't do it.

EXT. SHIP CHANNEL BANK - NIGHT
Fog. The sound of water. Lapping at the hull of a boat. The mist drfits, revealing...
Eyes. They are blue. The heavy brows above them dark gold, matted and damp.

CARL (O.S.)
My batteries are drawed down, both of 'em. ALternator belts were loose.
PULL BACK to see him. With his keroses lantern and his air horn.

KABUO (O.S.)
No sweat. We'll pull one a mine, get ya started.
PULL BACK to see him now, leaning on his gaff. Squinting up. At the top of Carl's
mast. We follow his gaze to see...

KABUO (O.S.)
You lashed up a lantern? 'Gainst a fog like this?
See it now. SWAYING as the helpless boat bobs in the night.

CARL (O.S.)
Lantern and a air horn. That's all I got, without my juice.

INT. CARL'S CABIN - LATER
CLOSE on a battery well. One battery sits in place, one spot is empty. And...
...CRASH! The butt end of a fishing gaff BANGS against the metal flange. Again.
Again. AGAIN. And as the next blow is STRUCK, the huge hand...
...slips, and the soft metal SLICES Carl's flesh across his palm.
He stops. Then SMASHES away, twice more. We PULL BACK to see...
...two batteries lie above the well. Carl sucks the blood from his cut. Then lifts Kabuo's
D-6 into place...

CARL

Don't know how long it's take to get a charge...

KABUO
Keep it tonight. We'll catch fish.
I'll see ya back on the docks...
Kabuo takes his gaff. Heedless of Carl's blood on the butt end.
Carl looks up, still crouching above his well.
CARL (quietly)
Hold on. You know as well as
I do, we got somethin' to talk about.
No response from Kabuo. He stands above the larger man. Silent, neutral. Waiting.

CARL
Seven acres. I'm wonderin' what you'd pay for 'em. Just curious, is all.

KABUO
What are you sellin' 'em for?
Why don't we start there.
Which makes the big man smile. Just a little.

CARL
Did I say I was selling? But if I was, I'd have to figure you want 'em real bad. Oughta
charge a sall fortune, maybe...
A slight shrug. Of giant shoulders.

CARL
Then again. Maybe you'd want your battery back.
Kabuo doesn't grin back. His face shows nothing at all.

KABUO
The battery's in, that's done with. Besides, you'd do the same for m...

CARL
...<u>might</u> do the same. I have to warn you 'bout that, chief. I'm not screwed together like
I used to be.
Kabuo's face remains impassive. Patient. And the big man squints up into it. Holding a
handkerchief to his injured hand.

CARL
Hell, I'm sorry, okay? About the whole damn mess. If I'd a been around, my mother
wouldn't a pulled it off that way.
He is sorry. And with that, Kabuo's face eases. Becomes like
Carl's own.
CARL (grins)
I was out there at sea. Fightin' you Jap sons-a-bitches.
KABUO (no grin)

I'm an American. Did I call you a Nazi, you big Nazi bastard?
CARL (softly)
Not that I recall.

KABUO
I killed men who looked just like you, pig-fed German bastards. And their blood don't wash off so easy.
Still no smile. Carl staring up.

KABUO
So don't talk to me about Japs, you big Nazi son of a bitch.
Carl laughs. And Kabuo chuckles, right along with him. Having kept his poker face the longer.

CARL
I am a bastard. I'm a big Hun
Nazi son of a bitch. And I still got your bamboo fishing rod.

KABUO
Oh, yeh?

CARL
Hid it from my mom. Caught a mess a sea runs. Damn thing's still in my closet.
KABUO (very softly)
You can have it. The hell with it.
The look between them now. Is very wonderful. In the subtlety of its connection.

CARL
$1200 an acre, that's what I paid
Ole, won't take a dime less. You got no choice on that.

KABUO
Didn't say I was buyin' did I?
What you want down? Just bein' curious, is all.
The handkerchief comes away from Carl's palm. And rising, his hand extends toward the smaller man.

CARL
A thousand down. We'll sign papers t'morrow.
The hands grip. And they hold. And the length of this clasp, and the straightness of their gaze, and the silence of the moment.
Wash years away.

KABUO
Eight hundred. And it's a deal.

INT. COURTROOM - DAY
CLOSE on eyes. They are Asian. Unblinking.

HOOKS (O.S.)
For the life of me, sir, I cannot <u>imagine</u> why you kept this story from the sheriff.
PULL BACK to see Kabuo in the witness box. Ramrod straight. Face composed.

KABUO
As my wife testified, we were considering it.

HOOKS
Actually, she said you had decided.
Decided <u>not</u> not come forward.
KABUO (quietly)
I was thinking about it. Every minute.

HOOKS
Except even when Sheriff Moran <u>arrested</u> you. You said <u>nothing</u> about seeing Carl.
Turns to the jury. Openly bewildered.

HOOKS
At that point, you were <u>already</u> under suspicion. The battery story <u>explained</u> things. If
the story was true...and not simply something you thought up later...
Turns back. To the defendant.

HOOKS
Why. Didn't you. Tell it?
No reaction from the defendant. Nothing anyone can see.

KABUO
Sheriff said right off, I was under suspicion. I didn't have a lawyer...

HOOKS
But even <u>after</u> you had an attorney. You still claimed to know <u>nothing</u>. Claimed <u>not</u> to
have seen Carl. Am I correct?
A beat.

KABUO

Yes. Initially.

HOOKS
Well, 'initially' is an interesting word, sir. You'd <u>been</u> arrested, you <u>had</u> a lawyer, and
you <u>still</u> claimed ignorance!
Silence.

KABUO

I should have told everything right away. I know that now, and I regret it.

HOOKS

Should have told 'everything'.
Meaning, you should have told the <u>truth</u>.
We can just discern the anger. At the edge of Kabuo's steady gaze.
Silence.

HOOKS

Nothing to say?
KABUO (quietly)
I didn't know that was a question.
It sounded like a speech.
And Hooks smiles. Loving it. Walks toward the witness, stalking him.

HOOKS

My apologies. Do you regret not telling the truth?

KABUO

I have told the truth.

HOOKS

You mean, this morning. The new story, the battery story.
That one is the truth? That's a question, sir.
KABUO (even quieter)
Yes. And I told it long before this morning.

HOOKS

I see. Now what happened the day Carl Heine was found? Before your arrest.

KABUO

I slept til one-thirty, when my wife woke me up with the news. We talked for a few hours. I left at six and went straight to my boat.

HOOKS

Didn't go anywhere else? No errands, no purchases? Just straight to the boat. That's the truth.

KABUO

Yes.
Hooks leans over the box. Ever so slightly invading Kabuo's space.

HOOKS

Well, the sheriff found <u>two</u> batteries in your well. If you left one with Carl Heine, how is that possible?

KABUO
I had a spare battery in my shed.
I brought it down, and put it in just before the sheriff showed up.
Ah. I see.

HOOKS
Conveniently, in your shed. Only you didn't mention that a moment ago.
Why does this battery story change every time a new question is raised?
Kabuo looks at him, evenly.

KABUO
You asked if I went straight to the boat. I did. With the battery.
Hooks steps back. Looks the witness over.

HOOKS
You're a hard man to trust, sir.
You sit before us, with no expression, keeping a poker f...

NELS (O.S.)
Objection!

JUDGE
You know better than that, Mr.
Hooks. Either ask questions that count for something, or sit down and be done with it.
Silence. The judge staring hard. Hooks never flinching.

JUDGE
Shame on you.
Hooks turns his eyes to Kabuo. Stares him down, so the jury can watch Kabuo's
implacable stare in return. And softly...

HOOKS
I apologize to the court, for letting my feelings get the better of me.
Turns away.

HOOKS
No other questions. We'll go to summation.
As he returns to his table. As Kabuo steps down from the box.
We PAN...
...reporters' row. The boys are writing as fast as their hands can move. Only Ishmael is
not writing at all. He stares at the pad resting on hsi right knee. We CLOSE to see...
One word circled. The word 'lantern'.

INT. COURTROOM - LATER

Alvin Hooks stalks the jury box now. Prowls before them along the rail. As their eyes follow.

HOOKS
...believing that Etta Heine's son would <u>never</u> sell him the land. Land that in <u>his</u> mind, filtered through ancient rules of behavior handed down from his ancestors' culture, <u>belonged</u> to his family by right...
Stops. To make sure they understand.

HOOKS
His <u>only</u> choice to get the land would be to <u>eliminate</u> Carl Heine.
So that Ole Jurgensen would need a new buyer.
Pacing again, hand trailing along the rail...

HOOKS
In his mind. Seen through codes of revenge difficult for us to fathom, this was also the <u>only</u> way to <u>avenge</u> what he felt to be the grievous <u>dishonor</u> brought to his father, his family...
Raises his finger. This must be heard...

HOOKS
...to a thousand years of ancestry, in a foreign land we <u>still</u> find an enigma. Despite our recent bitter experience with its ways.
And stops once more. Places his hands on the rail.

HOOKS
Thus believing cold-blooded murder to be <u>justified</u>...he trailed Carl Heine... could hear his engine in the fog...and sounded his own horn, claiming distress.
Straightens up. Shakes his head, ever so slightly.

HOOKS
As Carl pulled alongside: 'Please,
Carl,' the defendant must have said.
'I am sorry for what has come between us, but adrift here in the fog, I <u>plead</u> for your help!'
Imagine. Imagine that.

HOOKS
And so this good man tied his boat fast, while his enemy <u>leaps</u> aboard, <u>striking</u> the treacherous blow he was trained to strike by his father's hand.
Counting off the facts. One finger at a time.

HOOKS
The feud over these seven acres had festered for eight <u>years</u>. He <u>argued</u> with Carl about buying the land <u>one week</u> before Carl was killed.

Carl's skull was crushed, and his blood is on a murder weapon with which the defendant is a deadly expert!
Spreads his arms. Wide.

HOOKS
And after a series of lies. The defendant at last admits he was there. Alone on the boat. In the fog. Carl Heine's blood on his fishing gaff.
A hush. A murmur...

HOOKS
My lord. My lord.
Looking into the eyes now. Of each man. Each woman.

HOOKS
Look clearly at the defendant.
See the truth self-evident in him.
And in the facts of this case.
And turns. So that they will follow his eyes to Kabuo's stone- hard gaze.

HOOKS
Look into his eyes, ladies and gentlemen, consider his face.
And ask yourself what your duty is as citizens of this community.

INT. COURTROOM - LATER
PAN the jury, slowly, as they hear...

NELS (O.S.)
...not a single witness has testified to anything that could suggest pre- meditated murder. Not in the days before Carl Heine's death...or at any time...has anyone described a murderous rage toward the deceased.
Nels stands very still. Hands resting on the rail. As calm and quiet as his adversary had been dramatic.

NELS
Etta Heine had cheated his family.
He had asked his childhood friend
Carl to sell him the land. And
Carl was considering it.
Leans forward. Just a little.

NELS
There is no evidence of anger at
Carl, much less rage, much less murderous rage. No reason for premeditation and no evidence of it. Anywhere.
He picks out a housewife. The youngest. Smiles sadly, wisely. As her grandfather might.

NELS

And yet the state is required to <u>prove</u> these things. Beyond. A reasonable. Doubt.
His eyes widen.

NELS

Can you seriously think there is <u>no</u> reasonable doubt? Why is <u>Kabuo's</u>
D-6 battery in <u>Carl's</u> well, if Carl was helping <u>him</u>?
Why?

NELS

Why isn't the blood on the gaff <u>more</u> consistent with Carl's <u>hand</u> wound than a <u>skull</u>
fracture? Given the absence of bone or brain tissue.
And now. he begins to pace, limping slightly, eyes down.

NELS

What Mr. Hooks asks you to believe is that <u>no</u> proof is needed. Against a man who
bombed Pearl Harbor.
Slow. Eyes on his feet.

NELS

Look at his face, the prosecutor said.
Presuming that you will see an enemy there. Treacherous by nature, by a thousand years
of something or other.
He stops. Looks at them.

NELS

An argument I find as despicable as it is dishonest and twisted and <u>insulting</u> to us all.
Mr. Miyamoto is a <u>much</u>-decorated <u>hero</u> of the United
States Army. For God's sake.
The feeling wells in te old man. It bleeds through the very quietness of his voice.

NELS

If someone said you should convict
Carl Heine. Or his lovely widow.
Of murder. Without proof. Because their ancestry is the same as
Hitler's. You would <u>spit</u> in his eye.
Yes, you would.

NELS

And every decent American. Would applaud you.
He leans his elbows on their rail. As if confiding to them across their backyard fence.

NELS

Now Kabuo Miyamoto did one thing wrong. He was afraid to trust us, at first. Afraid
that he would be crucified by prejudice. As Mr. Hooks is urging you to do.

Silence.

NELS
Well, we sent him. And his wife.
And thousands of Americans to concentration camps. They lost homes, belongings, everything.
We did that, folks. Can we now be unforgiving about his uncertainty?
His mistrust?
Looking in their eyes. As if waiting for an answer. They shift their weight, fidget beneath his gaze.

NELS
You may think this is a small trial.
In a small place. Well, it isn't.
He straightens his spine. Winces slightly, with the pain of it.

NELS
Every once in awhile. Somewhere in the world. Humanity goes on trial. And integrity. And decency.
Every once in awhile, common folks get called on to give the report card for the human race.
The eyes are watering. But the voice gains strength.

NELS
Now here in America. We relish those chances. Give us that one, we say. That's why we built this country in the first place.
One step back. Just above a whisper...

NELS
Be Americans. Make your children proud.

INT. COURTROOM - LATER
CLOSE on handcuffs SNAPPING into place. Sheriff Moran checks their snugness about Kabuo's wrists, as the crowd mills through the courtroom in the wake of adjournment. Grasping Kabuo's arm, Moran begins leading him toward a small doorway just at the rear of the witness box. But...
...someone is there. In the doorway. And Moran's grip tightens as they approach...

MORAN
I'm awful sorry, Ma'am, but you know I c...

HATSUE
What are you afraid of, Sheriff?
The edge on that, the ballsy undertone, throws him a little.

HATSUE

Am I going to slip him a weapon for a mad escape? Perhaps a kendo staff hidden in my dress?

MORAN
There's rules.

HATSUE
Well, please break them, then.
I won't keep you a moment.
And she reaches past him. To take her husband's hands. She looks in his eyes, as if they are alone.

HATSUE
I love you. And tomorrow, when
I make our bed. I'm setting out your pillow.
Tears just flood her eyes. Sudden, unbidden. She holds tight to her smile. And to his hands.
HATSUE (whispers)
You better be there.
He smiles. A lovely, easy, cowboy-American smile.

KABUO
Only if you ask me nice.
ANGLE...from the gallery. One man watches. Watches as a woman brings manicled hands to her lips. And walks quickly away...
...toward us. Straight toward us, in fact. And when she stands before us, her hands mangle her purse. The eyes are hollow, flint- edged.

HATSUE
Did you write that column?

ISHMAEL
I did. But the jury won't s...

HATSUE
It's not for the. They only get to convict him.
She arches her throat. As if facing a firing squad.

HATSUE
It's the judge who decides. If he'll hang.
He reaches. His fingertips find her shoulder. She does not resist his touch.
ISHMAEL (gently)
None of that is gonna ha...

HATSUE
You don't think he did this.

His hand comes away. From his heart...

ISHMAEL
I know he didn't.
She nods. Nods. Her eyes filling. Moving over his face.

HATSUE
Come to supper, tonight. My mother would be proud to have you with us.
He hears the emotion in her voice. He swallows hard.

ISHMAEL
I can't.
No, I can't.

ISHMAEL
Tell your mom. I want a rain check.

INT. KABUO'S CELL - NIGHT
Kabuo sits on the cot, the way we have always seen him. Alone in his mind. Footfalls.
Kabuo oblivious, far away. The door CLANGS open.

MORAN
You have a visitor, son.
Turns to the visitor...

MORAN
You said three minutes.

ISHMAEL
Won't take two.
And Moran leaves. The door CLANGS shut. They are alone. Only one man smiling...

KABUO
Please, sit down...
But the tall man doesn't. Doesn't move.

KABUO
She told me you're writing a column. We're very grateful.
Ishmael nods, awkwardly. Acknowledging this.

KABUO
She. Said you two go way back...
Ishmael stares into Kabuo's earnest smile.

KABUO
That's nice.

ISHMAEL
You said there was a lantern in his hand. When you found him in the fog.
Kabuo blinks. The man's tone is formal. As if the offer of friendliness is somehow
rejected.

ISHMAEL
And another one. Lashed to the mast?
Kabuo's own smile has faded. The mask has returned.

KABUO
That's right.

ISHMAEL
Two. Lanterns.
And Kabuo grins. In spite of himself.

KABUO
If I did the math right.
Ishmael leans back. Against the door.

ISHMAEL
It's the sheriff's math. I'm wondering about.

INT. SOMMENSEN'S WAREHOUSE - NIGHT
Blackness. The sound of wind. Of water lapping at wood. CLICK of a key, springing a
lock. The SCRAPE of a large PADLOCK sliding away. A door CREAKS open, and
from the sound of it, a large one.
Gray light seeps in.

MORAN (O.S.)
Blackmail. That's all it is.
See them now. Three SILHOUETTES framed in thr barn's open doorway.
Against the night sky.

ISHMAEL (O.S.)
I call it keeping your promise.
We said if I ever needed some cooperation from you...
A soft CLICK, and the LIGHTS go on. Such as they are. A few bare bulbs strung across
the rafters of this towering ramshackle enclosure. A 50-year-old mildewed barn, built
of creosoted timbers. This is a place for overhauling boats, with sea doors facing the
harbor.
Two BOATS are tied to wide-elbowed piers. We've seen them before.

MORAN

You threatened me, Chambers, pure and simple. And what idiot's gonna believe some
cock and bull story that I made a deal to keep stuff outta your paper? Not that anybody
reads your paper.
Abel Martenson leads the way. Along soaking planks.

ISHMAEL
Same idiots who'll believe you cracked this case. When I tell
'em you did.
Moran snorts. Points up to the cross spar, high on the mast of the first boat.

MORAN
See, no lantern.
ABEL (respectfully)
Sheriff? That's Miyamoto's boat.
Oh. Moran swings his gaze up to the second boat.
MORAN (quiet triumph)
No lantern there, neither.
Sure enough. No lantern on the cross spar. They keep walking.

MORAN
Never shoulda given you that inventory in the first place.

ISHMAEL
It's public record. If the public cares enough to read it.
They step across the gunnel. Onto Carl Heine's boat. Flashlights working against the
dim, eerie glow of distant bulbs, they enter
Carl's cabin.
Neat as a pin. Ishmael scans the floor.

ISHMAEL
You said there was a coffee c...
ABEL (sorry)
I picked it up.
And points to the cup. Sitting on the counter.

ABEL
It's the only thing I moved, I swear. It was right there.
The sheriff glares at the boy.

MORAN
You wanna see that in the papers?
Don't ever touch something at a cri...
And stops. Because Ishmael's gaze has gone to a kerosene lantern.
In the corner.

MORAN

One lantern. Like the inventory says. Sorry to disappoint you.
But Ishmael is out the door. Shining his flashlight. Up the mast.

ISHMAEL
Actually. I was hoping you got it right. What's that, up there?
And they all squint up. Shining their lights together. Along the cross spar.

MORAN
Nothin'. Bits of string.
That's what it looks like. Many of them.

ISHMAEL
Pieces of twine aren't nothing.
And he steps to the base of the mast. Puts the flashlight in his pocket. Wraps his arm
around the shaft of wood.

MORAN
Here now, what are you fixin' to do?

ISHMAEL
Have a look. At nothing.
And wrapping his legs around the mast, he hoists himself up.

MORAN
You can't go up there, touch things...
With all his strength. Ishmael begins to climb.
ISHMAEL (grunting)
Trial's over, Sheriff, it's with the jury now.
Supporting himself with his legs, he struggles upward.

MORAN
You gonna climb that with one arm?

ISHMAEL
You're right. I better use two.
Up he goes, inching his way, Abel shining his flashlight. Moran swings his beam up,
too.

ABEL
There's lots of 'em, Art, look.
And Moran is looking. Saying nothing. Now, Ishmael is there.

ISHMAEL
A dozen or more, all figure eights.
All cut clean through on an angle.

ABEL
And look at that streak of rust, across the mast.
His light playing on it. Bracing his full weight with his legs,
Ishmael fingers the scraps of rope...

ISHMAEL
It's on the twine, too. But it's not r...

MORAN
Don't prove there was two lanterns.
Coulda been the one in the cabin.
Still supporting himself with his legs, Ishmael pulls out his flashlight...

ISHMAEL
There's a stretch of ground between guessin' and provin',
Sheriff. I'll give you that.
...shines it DOWN on the deck. Along the gunnel. Just below the mast. And as we watch
the circle of light move...

MORAN (O.S.)
What do you think you're lookin' at now?
Still moving. And in the silence, an absent...

ISHMAEL (O.S.)
Not what I'm looking at. It's what I'm looking for.

INT. JURY ROOM - NIGHT
Eleven citizens around a walnut table. Eleven. Glaring at the twelfth.

ALEXANDER VAN NESS
Well. I guess it comes down to a feeling, don't it? If I _feel_ uncertain, I feel a _doubt_. Isn't
that it?
And the boat builder smiles amicably, rubs his gray beard. No other smiles. Anywhere.

HAROLD JENSEN
Alex, nobody ain't ever _sure_ about nothin'. It's _unreasonable_ to be so stubborn that you
think you're smarter than _eleven_ folks who all _agree_!

EDITH TWARDZIK
The man sat there and _admitted_ he _lied_, Mr. Van Ness. Now _why_ isn't that enough for
you?

ALEXANDER VAN NESS
We're not tryin' him for lying. Lots of us told lies, one time or another.
Prob'ly none of us murdered anybody.

HAROLD JENSEN
But what <u>drives</u> a man to lie?
Means he's <u>hiding</u> somethin'.

ALEXANDER VAN NESS
Not <u>necessarily</u> that he killed
Carl. I'm not sayin' you're wrong, just that I have my doubts.

BURKE LATHAM
Look, if you changed chairs right now, cos you doubted that maybe a chunk of the moon
was gonna fall through the roof, that wouldn't be a <u>reasonable</u> doubt.
Folks turn to Burke. What the hell are you talking about?
ALEXANDER VAN NESS (laughs)
Okay, you win that one. Now can we all go to bed?
HARLAN McQUEEN
The mooring line. Doesn't that tell you something?

ALEXANDER VAN NESS
I think it does. Miyamoto was on
Carl's boat, or vice-versa. Not much doubt about th...
MARLAN McQUEEN
And Carl's blood on the gaff?

ALEXANDER VAN NESS
There's a chance it came from his hand.

BURKE LATHAM
There's a chance of everything.
But you add a chance from here and a chance from there, the world ain't made a
coincidences only.
Everyone agrees. Almost everyone.

EDITH TWARDZIK
Look, if he gave Carl a battery like he said, he'd only a had <u>one</u> left. Not two.

ALEXANDER VAN NESS
He explained that. He replaced it.
HARLAN McQUEEN
Only he threw that part in when he got cornered. But first time around, he never
mentioned it.

ROGER PORTER
Alex, stop arguin' just to argue.
You can see what <u>really</u> happened, same as us. Isn't that what we're supposed to do is
tell the actual truth? My God, Carl died, here.

ALEXANDER VAN NESS
So I don't care Carl died, unless
I'm ready to reach for the hangman's rope? You oughta stop tryin' to bully me into
hurrying.
Little anger in that. It brings a silence.

BURKE LATHAM
Been six hours. You sayin' there's a way to go slower?

INT. NELS' KITCHEN - LATE NIGHT
Nels in a ratty, frayed old robe, pouring hot water from a kettle into mismatched cups.
His hair is wispy and wild, his eyes puffy.
He COUGHS horrible. CLEARS his throat...

NELS
Well. It's imaginative...
And drops tea bags into the cups with a splash.

NELS
...I'll give you that.
Lisps over to the cluttered table. Where his guest is waiting.

ISHMAEL
It's the way it happened, I know it is.

NELS
No, you don't.
Nels sits. Slowly. Ishmael removes his bag. Sips his tea.

NELS
That report. About the freighter?
You didn't find that tonight, did you?
No answer. Ishmael keeps sipping. Holding eye contact.

NELS
You went right to the cell. Then to the boat. Then here. How long did you know about
the freighter?
ISHMAEL (just above a whisper)
One day.
Nels' turn. To sip his tea.

NELS
This tastes horrible, hmmn?

ISHMAEL
You're wondering why I held it.

NELS

I'm wondering how the judge is gonna like my waking up his old bones. in the middle of the night.
And he smiles. A wonderful smile.

NELS

Your daddy. Was quite a feller.

ISHMAEL

Yes, he was.
Another sip.

NELS

He's looking down. And he's not thinking 'bout the man you were yesterday. He's proud of the man you are tonight. That's what counts.

ISHMAEL

To my father. Everything counts.
Nels watches the pain in that.

NELS

What if I told you he once said to me...don't matter the road we take. Just so we get there.
ISHMAEL (smiles)
Then you'd be lying.

NELS

Doesn't make me wrong.

INT. COURTROOM - DAY

The jury once more in the jury box. PAN their faces. The faces we saw last night.

NELS (O.S.)

All right, let's say that twine <u>had</u> been there to lash a lantern.
That it had come from the shuttle of twine found in the deceased's pocket.
Edith Twardzik. Burke Latham. Alexander Van Ness.

NELS (O.S.)

Now to re-open a trial that had gone to jury...new evidence should be pretty important.
See Ishmael. Quiet, intense. On the witness stand.

NELS (O.S.)

Tell us why that lantern would be so significant.

ISHMAEL

Well. It shows the prosecutor was wrong. It was <u>Carl's</u> boat that was dead in the water.
Or he'd never have put up the lantern.
Nels thinks about that. So the jury will, too.

NELS
Now you believe there were <u>two</u> lanterns when defendant arrived.
One in Carl's hand. The second lashed to the mast.

ISHMAEL
That's what Mr. Miyamoto reported, and he'd have no reason to lie.
He couldn't know that it would help his case.

NELS
Well, why does it?

ISHMAEL
Because the second lantern, the one on the mast. Was never found. So we have to ask...
A slight shurg. Stating the obvious.

ISHMAEL
...where did it go?
And then...

ISHMAEL
Maybe it went. Where Carl went.
Over the side.

HOOKS
Objection! Speculation.
Nels smiles his grandfather smile.

NELS
Your Honor, <u>all</u> of this is speculation. Including Mr. Hooks' dramaturgy about the
defendant issuing a false distress call.

HOOKS
Tht was summation, Your H...
JUDGE (gently)
Overruled, Alvin. Let's hear this, hmmn?
Nels Gudmundsson nods to himself. Takes a stroll over to the jury box. No limp today.
Something has put some spring in his step.

NELS
So how does this fit with what you told us at the start? The freighter that plowed through
Ship Channel Bank...
And turns. Leaning his scrawny butt against the jury's rail.

He'll watch this with them now.

ISHMAEL
That's when he fell.

NELS
Fell.
Ishmael settles in. Here we go.

ISHMAEL
Miyamoto gave him the battery, and left. Carl's boat was running, he goes back to fishing. But at some point, he thinks of the lantern...

NELS
Still lashed to the mast.

ISHMAEL
He figures a perfectly good lantern could get banged around up there. So he climbs up. To cut it down.

NELS
Just as the freighter comes through?
Isn't that quite a coincidence?

ISHMAEL
Coincidences happen. You run a yellow light <u>just</u> as a car comes out of nowhere. Split-second tragedy happens every day. Or maybe...

NELS
Maybe...?

ISHMAEL
Maybe Carl picks up something about the freighter on his radio, which is now working. Same report Milholland heard. And <u>that</u> makes him get the lantern fast. Before the freighter's wake can bang it around.

NELS
But you <u>could</u> be wrong. He <u>could</u> have climbed up earlier.

ISHMAEL
Then where's the lantern? And where's the knife?

NELS
The knife. What knife?
As if he really has forgotten. As if he wants to know.

ISHMAEL
Coroner found an empty knife sheath on Carl's belt. But they never found the knife.
He's nodding. Yes, that's right.

ISHMAEL
He climbs up. His hand wound still bleeding. That's the blood I found on the mast. <u>And</u>
the twine.
Nels' eyes are rapt. His mouth is shut. No way he interrupts this roll.

ISHMAEL
He <u>cuts</u> the lantern free, the freighter's wake <u>hits</u>, the boat rolls <u>hard</u>, his bloody hand
<u>slips</u>. tracing blood along the mast...
A hush.

ISHMAEL
He falls. The lantern, the knife, go <u>into</u> the water. Same as Carl.
The words hang there.

ISHMAEL
And inside the cabin, a coffee cup falls off the counter.
Shakes his head.

ISHMAEL
But there's no one around. To pick it up.
Nels ponders. Puts his hand to his chin.

NELS
Still a coincidence. Timing and all.

ISHMAEL
The freighter started through at 1:42. The sea water seeped into Carl's watch and stopped
it.
At 1:47.
CUT to the defendant. Ramrod straight, nothing revealed in his face. And to his wife.
Elegant, erect. Her eyes flooded with tears.

NELS
Still and all. Carl was a strong swimmer, he m...

ISHMAEL
He hit his head. On the way in.
Silence.

NELS
You think so?

ISHMAEL

The sheriff and the deputy and I inspected the deck closely. We found a small fracture in the wood of the gunnel. Just below the mast.

NELS

Well, anything coulda caused that.
Ishmael nods. No smile at all.

ISHMAEL

Anything. That had a blond hair.
And Nels is walking now. Toward the prosecutor's table. Pulling a small cellophane bag from hisinside pocket.

NELS

Request introduction of Exhibit 18.
One single blond hair. Which Sheriff
Moran dug out of that fracture. Below the mast. Of Carl Heine's boat.
Lays the bag on the table. Just in front of Hooks. Turns to the judge.

NELS

We will call Sheriff Moran, who will confirm this. And Coroner
Whaley to testify that the damage to the gunnel is of a size and nature not inconsistent with the deceased's skull fracture...
Turns to the prosecutor...

NELS

But for now. Your witness...
And just strolls on over to his seat. Looks in his client's eyes.
How 'bout them apples? Kabuo loves this old guy. And right here, he lets a little of that show.
Across the way, the prosector is rising. He smiles. Friendly, almost amused.

HOOKS

I have to start reading your paper more closely. You're quite a storyteller.
ISHMAEL (straight back)
Thank you. Coming from the man who wrote, 'But here, adrift in the fog,
I <u>plead</u> for your help'...that's quite a compliment.
There is a ripple of laughter. But no smile on Ishmael's features.
His game face is on. Come and get me, sucker. And Hooks does come, one step at a time. Straight to the box.

HOOKS

<u>Everything</u> had to happen <u>just</u> right. For your little story to fly. I mean, a blond hair could be on that gunnel for a <u>lot</u> of reasons.

ISHMAEL

I'm sorry, was there a question in there?
No love lost. And no pretense about it. Hatsue Miyamoto sits with her hand in her mother's. Watching these men battle for her husband's life.

HOOKS
Well, the freighter. The twine.
The blood. The knife. The cup.
The watch. The second battery.
The phantom lantern. The fishing gaff. The cracked gunnel. The skull wound. The blond hair. That's <u>eleven</u> things...

ISHMAEL
Twelve.
Hooks smiles.

HOOKS
I stand corrected, sir. And you have a neat explanation for every one of them.
Hooks nods. Yes, you do.

HOOKS
And since you confess this is all pure guesswork. What is your expertise, sir, are you a detective of sorts?

ISHMAEL
My expertise. Is that I'm a journalist.
Right at his eyes.

ISHMAEL
And journalism. Is balance. Finding the facts folks need to know.
The words ring with quiet, heartfelt conviction, that others cannot fully appreciate.

ISHMAEL
Then putting them together. So truth is revealed.

HOOKS
But isn't the <u>truth</u> that there are <u>several</u> other ways to explain <u>each</u> of these twelve pieces.

ISHMAEL
Oh, yes.
And the prosecutor stops. Confused for an instant by this confession. Until...

ISHMAEL
But <u>no</u> other way. To explain them all.
A heart-stopping hush. As everyone, as Hooks himself, sees the cehckmate.

ISHMAEL

And since they <u>all</u> happened.
This is the only explanation that's the truth.
The prosecutor looks like he's been slapped. Like every act of will is necessary to maintain composure. To find the easy, untroubled smile.

HOOKS
Your line of work. You must meet a lot of men play fast and loose with the truth.

ISHMAEL
Like you couldn't believe.
Service returned. Hooks leans in.

HOOKS
Well, the defendant is a liar.
He's confessed that much. And his explanation is...he was afraid.
And leans in some more.

HOOKS
Afraid that the good folks of this jury. Would be too stupid to understand. Too prejudiced to be fair.
Shakes his head.

HOOKS
You buy that?
ISHMAEL (gently)
I think he was greedy.
And once more. The prosecutor can only blink. Can only move toward the trap.

HOOKS
Greedy.

ISHMAEL
He didn't want to lose any more.
No smile. No smile as the trap springs shut.

ISHMAEL
He'd lost a lot in the war, you see. I had sent him away. To a concentration camp. But a nice one. <u>Far</u> less brutal than the Nazis.
Because I'm a civilized person.
He stops. Lets Hooks clear his throat.

HOOKS
I asked you a question, you're writing a tract, h...

ISHMAEL
That's how journalists. Answer questions.

Turns to Judge Fielding. With all respect...

ISHMAEL
May I answer the question, Your
Honor? Anout the defendant's motivation to lie?

JUDGE
I wouldn't miss it for the world, son. Now, you say <u>you</u> sent the defendant to Manzanar?

ISHMAEL
I didn't say. I did it alone.
And things get real quiet.

ISHMAEL
So there he was. His father lost his health there, finally died.
They lost more than Etta Heine's seven acres. They lost their liberty, their dignity. Their
ideals about this country.
So much feeling in this. He has to stop. Swallow hard.

ISHMAEL
They lost their trust in us. We had treated them worse than animals.
How would we now see tham. As human beings?
Tells the jury. Straight to their faces.

ISHMAEL
This man lost a lot in the war.
He didn't want now to lose his babies. Or the woman who loves him.
Another level of quiet. He turns to the prosecutor...

ISHMAEL
And my expertise in this, sir. Is that I lost a lot in the war myself.
Words coming from someplace very deep.

ISHMAEL
And the fact that I am the only witness. Who placed his <u>right</u> hand upon the Holy Bible.
Is the <u>least</u> of it, sir. I assure you of that.
Silence.

HOOKS
Well, sir. I hate to spoil the soliloquy, I truly do. But the fact is...you are not on trial
here.
Nor is Judge Fielding, or myself.
Nor the good people of this jury.
For events that took place twelve years ago.
No sir.

HOOKS

And I wouldn't blame these good people if they were a mite resent- ful. At a tactic that insults their intelligence.

ISHMAEL

That's curious. I was <u>appealing</u> to their intelligence.

HOOKS

<u>Were</u> you, sir? Can you <u>prove</u> one word of all your fancy story?

ISHMAEL

No, sir, I can't. Not beyond a reasonable doubt.
And he smiles. First time.

ISHMAEL

It's fortunate that the man who <u>needs</u> to prove <u>his</u> fancy story.
Beyond a reasonable doubt. Is someone else.
There is laughter in the room, so welcome is any chance to relieve the tension. The gavel BANGS.

ISHMAEL

I'm sorry, Mr. Hooks. I apologize for my tone. This is not a contest.
Between you and me.
Shakes his head. No, it isn't.

ISHMAEL

For it is not. As Mr. Gudmundsson so wisely put it. A small trial.
In a small place.
His eyes are damp now. Strangely enough, after all this. He is at last on the brink of losing control. Because...

ISHMAEL

I lost more in that war than anyone will ever know. So did a lot of folks. And what we got back in return...
His voice breaks slightly. But it rings with dignity on...

ISHMAEL

...was a country. Where a man was innocent. Until we <u>proved</u> him guilty.
And the voice drops. To just above a whisper...

ISHMAEL

Whether we all got cheated.
We're about to find out.

INT. COURTHOUSE CORRIDOR - DAY

CLOSE on Hatsue Miyamoto, speaking earnestly, her eyes down, her purse in her lap, her slender hands expressing the intensity of her feelings as she makes her point, and we...

PULL BACK to reveal that she is on a corridor bench, surrounded by a half dozen REPORTERS, who are crouching, standing, scribbling away. Two PHOTOGRAPHERS pop flashes that she does not seem to notice, as she continues with refined determination, and we...

PULL BACK, down the hallway to the POV of a man who sits alone, unnoticed. There is an unopened pack of cigarettes in his only hand, turning absently in long, strong fingers that crinkle the pristine cellophane. His eyes are fixed to hatsue, holding court at a distance. Fixed, as if no other sight could ever command this level of attention.

NELS (O.S.)
All things considered...
Hearing the voice, Ishmael looks down. Uneasy to have been caught staring so intently.

NELS
...you were adequate.
No smile accompanies the irony. For that would be condescending.

NELS
I could make a few quibbles, but
I am loathe to hurt your feelings.
The old man sits. Very slowly.

ISHMAEL
Cigarette?

NELS
I'll take two. One for later.
Ishmael tries to tear the cellophane without success. Nels seems not even to notice.
NELS (quietly)
She is simply. Beautiful.
Ishmael's eyes cut to him. A little quickly. Confides...

ISHMAEL
I've always thought so.
There it sits. His fingers claw absently at the cellophane. Nels makes no move to intervene.

NELS
If I whistle. Those boys'll see you, and come runnin'. <u>You're</u> the story today.

ISHMAEL
You ever been strangled by a single hand?

NELS
Naw, I've seen what that can do to a pack of cigarettes.
Comfortable together. In this hour of discomfort. Ishmael brings the corner of the pack
to his teeth, and tears the cellophane away.

ISHMAEL
Better take three...
Fingers nimbly shred the seal, open the pack.

ISHMAEL
Maybe they'll keep us waiting.
Shake the tips free. Holds the pack forward.
NELS (very quiet)
Maybe they won't.
The way he said that. Subtly ominous. Ishmael watching Nels' face, as the old man takes
two cigarettes...

NELS
Prejudice is like any obsession.
Tucks one in his pocket. And his eyes slide, unmistakably, to
Hatsue.

NELS
There's a reason why we can't let go. Even when we want to.
Ishmael is stone still. Nels just gazing at Hatsue. Until...

ISHMAEL
A reason.
NELS (simply)
We don't want to.
Looks back to Ishmael. Very straight.

NELS
Hate or love. It works the same.
In the silence...

ISHMAEL
Your client's wife ever mention?
We go way ba...
NELS (softly)
Her mother. May have said something.
There it is. Kindness in this old man's face. He brings the other cigarette to his lips. And
Ishmael takes out the match box. Never breaking eye contact.

ISHMAEL
We don't let go, you s...

NELS

It's a rare thing. Takes a turning point.
Expertly, Ishmael's fingers withdaw a match.

NELS

You gave this jury three chances.
To turn.
Palming the box, Ishmael STRIKES the match. On his belt buckle...

NELS

<u>No</u> other way to explain it <u>all</u>.
That was one. I caught some of 'em fluttering, waking up, on that.
Reaches the flame toward the old man...

NELS

Second. <u>You</u> sent him to
Manzanar, and you didn't do it <u>alone</u>. I liked that one, they didn't. No surprise.
Nels leans to the flame. Sucks it in. Savors a drag.

NELS

Last. You gave your arm. To buy this woman back her husband.
Are they gonna cheat you out of that?
BAILIFF (O.S., calling out)

JURY'S COMIN' IN...

Everywhere, the buzz RISES, there is motion an expectation. But
Nels doesn't seem to notice.

NELS

Some let go, some don't. Where did you?
Asked so casually. Ishmael turns. Hatsue is standing now, surrounded by people, her
mother grasping her arm.
ISHMAEL (a murmur)
Hooks called her deceitful.
And I knew she wasn't.
He's watching her. Across the way. So intently.

ISHMAEL

She was an honest person. Doing the best she could.
We follow her approach toward the courtroom door. She has not yet turned to us.

NELS (O.S.)

The prosecutor, the judge, cut her off. She was desperate. Her husband helpless...I was
helpless...
Nels rises. With great effort.

NELS
You couldn't let her. Be helpless.
Ishmael's eyes still fixed to Hatsue, grim-faced, listening to her mother's murmurings,
as she...
...disappears through the door. Never having looked our way.

NELS
When this verdict is read. She may look for your face.
And Ishmael's eyes come up. Because the voice commands it.

NELS
Here's what she needs to see: This is nothing. We win it on appeal.
The old man is stern and strong. He wants a promise.

ISHMAEL
It'll be there.

INT. COURTROOM - DAY
The hush of a hundred silences. We can feel the air crackle in the stillness. Judge
Fielding is leafing through papers. No one coughs, no one blinks...
JUDGE (clears his throat)
Mister foreman, has the jury reached a verdict?
He looks up. Across the distance, Harold Jensen rises in the jury box.

HAROLD JENSEN
We have, Your Honor.
And holds out a slip of paper. Little more than a scrap. Folded once.

JUDGE
Will the bailiff please bring the verdict to the bench.
The bailiff does so, walking crisply to minimize his moment in the limelight. He hands
the slip to the judge, who unfolds it, and...
...stops. Staring for a hung instant. As if seeing something unexpected. he folds it again,
rather carefully, thoughtfully, and as he hands it back to the bailiff...
JUDGE (softly)
Will the defendant please rise.
Kabuo and Nels rise together. But it is only into the defendant's eyes that the judge
stares. No expression in the face of either man. But something passes, all the same.
As the bailiff crosses to return the verdict to the foreman, we

SNAP TO...
REVERSE ANGLE...every pair of eyes in the room are on the foreman, now opening
the slip of paper.
Every pair. But one.

JUDGE (O.S.)
Will the foreman please read the verdict aloud.
One reporter stares across the grain of all other sight lines.
Toward a woman who does not see him. In case she needs his eyes.
To be waiting.
HAROLD JENSEN (reads)
We the jury, find the defendant,
Kabuo Kenji Miyamoto, to be not guilty of the cri...
A sharp SCREAM, and the defendant's mother-in-law covers her mouth in embarrassment.
HAROLD JENSEN (continues)
...of the crime with which he has been char...
APPLAUSE breaks out from the back row of the gallery, where citizens of Japanese ancestry have forgotten custom and decorum, as has...
...a woman who comes OUT of her seat, tears on her face, not even realizing she is standing, Hatsue clings to the railing that separates her from her husband. Throughout the gallery, now...
...some of the citizens assembled add their applause. Others look awkward, not knowing how to react.
The gavel lies untouched, unnoticed, by a jurist who has no problem with anything that is taking place right now. Saying only to the jury...

JUDGE
This is your verdict, so say you all?
As they assent...

JUDGE
This Court thanks you for the good work you have done under difficult circumstances...
Reaches STRONG to the gavel, turns to the defendant...

JUDGE
Go home, son. God bless.
CRACKS the gavel on its block. The defendant is OUT of his chair, and with one strong grip of gratitude to the frail shoulder of his counsel, he is...
...AT the rail, through the POPPING of flashbulbs, she is IN his arms, the embrace so FIERCE on both sides, everyone crowding around them.
An old man's eyes sweep the gallery, looking for someone. Only to find...
...Ishmael's back. As he disappears through the door.

INT. COURTHOUSE CORRIDOR - LATER
The Miyamotos holding court, surrounded by nearly twenty reporters and photographers, and countless looky-loo's of all persuasions.
Hatsue's face is flushed and intense, unsmiling, she seems scarcely to have caught her breath. She holds tight to her husband's hand, as he...
...carries his baby son in the other arm, his 8-year-old daughter leaning against him, her 4-year-old sister standing on the bench beside her mom. Kabuo submits to questions

with a boyish grin of humility and friendliness. An American family. Photogenic as hell.

REPORTER #1
And how about the jury? You had confidence they'd see justice done?
Kabuo glances to his lawyer, wanna field this one? But Nels sends it back with a twinkle.

KABUO
Oh, sure. These are our neighbors, you know. They've got good hearts. We could see they were following the evidence real close...
At his side, Hatsue seems to be scanning the jumble of faces...

KABUO
We're just grateful to every one of them.
...looking for something she doesn't find.

REPORTER #2
And you ma'am? You felt the same as your husband, I expect?
Her eyes move to the eager young man. She reflects for a beat.

HATSUE
Honestly, no.
Which catches everyone. A little short.
HATSUE (quietly)
I felt my husband would be found guilty. Unless proven innocent.
No apologies for the truth. That's not her way.

HATSUE
And Mr. Chambers did that.

INT. COURTHOUSE BASEMENT
A vending machine stands in silence. The eerie strobing glow of defective neon. PULL BACK as...
Ishmael thinks it over. Drops in his dime. Pulls the plunger, to watch a Snickers fall. Scoops the candy from the tray, pins it between his body and the machine.
...tears the wrapper.

INT. COURTHOUSE CORRIDOR
BACK to the reporters. The crowd of onlookers has grown.

REPORTER #3
...can we get some background on your handsome family? I understand you two were childhood sweethearts...
And brings his Parker pen to his notepad. His subject smiles easily...

KABUO

Well, no sir, not exactly. We met in the Manzanar camp, you see, so I guess that was the most beautiful place I've ever been.

There is gentle laughter. And as Kabuo looks up, he sees something in the rear of the crowd. Something we do not. And softly...

KABUO

No, her first love was another fella...

Which brings Hatsue's eyes up, following his gaze. And there, in the back. A man watches. Eating a candy bar.

KABUO (O.S.)

I was the lucky one.

No one sees their eyes lock. It is only an instant.

It is enough.

REPORTER #4

It all sounds very romantic, ma'am. Falling in love under those circumstances...

And as she looks to the reporter, Ishmael begins to walk away...

HATSUE

He went off to the Army, right from Manzanar. And that last night, we danced alone in the desert...

And somehow, Ishmael catches the eye of Hatsue's 4-year-old daughter. So he pulls a coin from his pocket...

HATSUE (O.S.)

I told him. If you don't come back alive, I'll kill you.

...Ishmael ROLLS the coin across his knuckles. And the child responds...

With her mother's smile.

EXT. COURTHOUSE STEPS - DUSK

Alone on the steps where the Strawberry Princess once winked at him. Snow has begun to fall, soft and altogether beautiful. He squints up...

ISHMAEL (V.O.)

God's kindness, my father said.

Despite the hardship...it reminds us. Of our place in things.

Our place in things. He slides a black cigar between his teeth...

ISHMAEL (V.O.)

What the hell. Did he mean by that?

He has the match box. Manipulating it with the dexterity we've come to know.

ISHMAEL (V.O.)

Things fall on us, I suppose.

From the sky.
STRIKES the match on his belt buckle...

ISHMAEL (V.O.)
Wars. Freighters plowing through...
Cupping it expertly in a single motion, he brings the flame to the cigar. A single puff.

ISHMAEL (V.O.)
And we seem...helpless. Until we understand.
One more. Savors it. The sky. The thought.

ISHMAEL (V.O.)
Accident rules every corner of the universe...
Down the steps. Snow swirling between us. Gone.

ISHMAEL (V.O.)
Except the chambers. Of the human heart.

FADE SLOWLY TO BLACK. ROLL END CREDITS.

www.ingramcontent.com/pod-product-compliance
Lightning Source LLC
Chambersburg PA
CBHW080906160726
48000CB00009B/2879